super **salads**

super salads

michael van straten

MITCHELL BEAZLEY

Super Salads

by Michael van Straten

First published in Great Britain in 2002 by
Mitchell Beazley, an imprint of Octopus Publishing
Group Limited, 2–4 Heron Quays, London E14 4JP.

A CIP catalogue record for this book is available from the British Library.

ISBN: 1 84000 551 3

The author and publishers will be grateful for any information which will assist them in keeping
future editions up to date. Although all reasonable care has been taken in the preparation of this
book, neither the publishers nor the author can accept any liability for any consequences arising
from the use thereof, or the information contained therein.

Commissioning editors: Rebecca Spry, Hilary Lumsden
Executive art editor: Yasia Williams
Photographer: Nicki Dowey
Designer: Peter Dawson
Editor: Jamie Ambrose
Production: Alexis Coogan
Index: Laura Hicks

Typeset in Myriad MM

Printed and bound by Toppan Printing Company in China

Contents

Introduction

Contrary to popular opinion, salads are not "boring". Good salads are delicious combinations of vegetables, fruits, nuts, seeds, eggs, fish, shellfish, beans, rice, couscous, and pasta. Flavoured with fresh herbs, spiced with chillies, and tossed in delicate dressings, they can be a meal in themselves – and one of the healthiest meals at that.

Super Salads is just what it says: a book filled with super, healthy salads. The recipes vary from simple dishes prepared in minutes to more adventurous ones that take rather longer. Either way, your efforts will be handsomely rewarded. Each super salad is delicious to eat and has a specific health-giving benefit that will contribute to overall well-being. For example, when the next flu epidemic strikes, choose a salad to boost your natural immunity. There are also recipes to cleanse the system, stimulate circulation, restore vitality, build muscles, and strengthen bones. Trying to lose weight? Here you'll find tasty, imaginative salads that are low in calories and saturated fats, and packed with ingredients designed to stimulate your metabolism and whittle away those surplus pounds.

The dishes in *Super Salads* will help improve your skin and restore it to glowing vitality. If the winter blues are getting you down, then munch your way through mood-changing and warming winter salads. Finally, if your sex life is flagging, don't fret: I've included some choice morsels designed to increase desire and improve performance.

After forty years as a naturopath, osteopath, and acupuncturist, I've learned many things from my patients. Since nutritional therapy is the basic platform of holistic healing, our discussions frequently centre on food, and many of the recipe ideas in this book have been garnered from patients from all around the world. Yet the most important lesson I've learned is that you can talk to people about healthy eating until you're blue in the face, but unless the food tastes good, then you're wasting your breath. I promise that every recipe* in *Super Salads* tastes delicious, and is beneficial to your health.

*Unless otherwise specified, each salad recipe serves four people.

Michael's standard salad dressing

Of course, any successful salad depends as much on the dressing as it does on the ingredients. Below is a basic recipe for my favourite dressing, which you can make in advance and keep in a dark, tightly stoppered bottle. Make any quantity you like, as long as the proportions are the same. This makes one imperial pint (600ml or 20fl oz) and is perfect for any sort of salad. Many recipes in this book specify other dressings, but you can use this one as an alternative. In addition to its wonderful taste, this dressing contains all the heart-protective benefits of olive oil, garlic, and onions, and the digestive benefits of cider vinegar, rosemary, and bay leaves.

400ml OR 14fl oz extra-virgin olive oil

200ml OR 7fl oz cider vinegar

1 tablespoon runny honey

1 tablespoon Dijon mustard

2 spring onions, finely chopped (including the green parts)

1 clove of garlic, finely chopped

Freshly ground black pepper

A sprig of fresh rosemary

2 bay leaves

Mix together all the ingredients except the rosemary and bay leaves in a jug and pour into a bottle (an empty Groslch bottle is ideal).

Add the rosemary and bay leaves and shake well before using.

lmm

unity
Salads

If we all lived in an ideal world, the air we breathe, the water we drink, the food we eat, and the environments in which we work and live would be free of the appalling chemical cocktail of pollutants that continuously assaults our immune systems. Yet the world is far from ideal, and the chemical onslaught extends right into our "personal space" on a daily basis.

You may think your home would provide a safe haven – but think again: immune-damaging chemicals lurk in the most unsuspected places. Volatile organic compounds are found in adhesives, paints, varnishes, and vinyl flooring. Hormone-disrupting phthalates inhabit plastic containers, food wraps, and many other types of plastic item. Toxic synthetic musks are common in washing powders, polishes, fabric softeners, and air fresheners, while lead residues, insecticides, and flame-retardants may all be found in the dust buried in the carpet. The dangers of pollutants extend to modern gardens, too, where deadly arsenic leaches out of preserved timber in decking, fence posts, and wooden playground equipment.

The potential damage from pollution is compounded by our lifestyles and attitudes to disease. Centuries before the discovery of antibiotics, human beings learned to use the resources of nature for protection against the hordes of invading bacteria and viruses that spread illness. There is no doubt that modern hygiene, water treatment, and sewage systems have eliminated some of the worst infectious diseases that afflicted mankind; it is also true that antibiotics have saved countless millions of lives. Yet in this most modern and high-tech of times, the germs are fighting back by becoming ever more resistant to modern, high-tech drugs.

To make matters worse, modern man has become so obsessed with hygiene and the frequent dowsing of every surface with antibacterial sprays that today's children are growing up with fewer challenges to their natural defence mechanisms. Without this natural stimulation, their immunity suffers, with the result that they become easy prey to opportunistic organisms.

Yet take heart: you *can* fight back. One effective way to combat the onslaught of pollution and strengthen your natural defences is by improving your diet. Immune-boosting foods will help encourage your body's natural resistance to pollution as well as to disease-causing bacteria – which is why the salads in this chapter provide a rich source of antioxidants and other phyto- (plant) chemicals that play a major part in protecting every human cell. In addition, they provide the equally essential vitamins A, C, and E, betacarotenes, including limonene, and vital minerals such as zinc. Adding herbs such as oregano and mint introduces an extra source of super-protection, thanks to the antibacterial essential oils they supply in such abundance.

By making these salads a regular part of your meal plan, you can help your body fight off infection and repair damage caused by a pollution-laden environment. They're as easy to make as they are delicious to eat, so what better way to take your (preventative) "medicine?"

A simple yet powerful dose of natural protection

Green-and-white delight

There's more than visual appeal to this simple but powerfully immune-boosting salad. Watercress belongs to the same valuable plant family as cabbages, broccoli, and Brussels sprouts. It contains some iodine, lots of potassium, and the strong mustard oil known as benzyl, which is an effective antibiotic.

Other natural chemicals found in watercress make it specifically protective against lung cancer. Combined here with the antibacterial, circulatory, and cholesterol-lowering properties of onions, this is a salad that should be eaten regularly – particularly by anyone still misguided enough to smoke.

1 large bunch of watercress

2 white onions

2 tablespoons extra-virgin olive oil

1 tablespoon walnut oil

Thoroughly wash the watercress – even if it's "ready-washed". Dry and pick off any very thick stalks.

Peel the onions and thinly slice.

Put the watercress into a bowl, then lay the onion slices on top.

Drizzle with each oil – and enjoy!

A sunny salad with an antibacterial punch

Viva España bread salad

Nothing could be quicker, easier, or more delicious than this typical Spanish salad, which I first ate at a hilltop *cantina* in the lovely mountain village of Frigiliana, in Andalucía. Followed by fresh fruit and a piece of cheese, it's an instant summer meal bursting with Mediterranean sunshine, but make it using only really ripe tomatoes and stale, coarse wholemeal or country bread.

Ripe tomatoes are rich in the essential nutrient lycopene, which protects against prostate and breast cancer as well as heart disease. The bread provides B vitamins and essential fibre; the onions and garlic help lower cholesterol and boost your natural immunity, as they contain both antibacterial and antifungal agents. Basil is one of the most calming and mood-enhancing of all the herbs, so adding it to this dish makes you feel good, too.

3 tablespoons extra-virgin olive oil

2 cloves of garlic, chopped

4 thick slices of bread, cubed (crusts removed)

6 ripe plum tomatoes

1 red onion, peeled and sliced

1 tablespoon lemon juice

A pinch of coarse sea salt

Freshly ground black pepper

1 handful of torn fresh basil leaves

Heat the oil in a frying pan and add the garlic and bread cubes. Stir until the bread becomes crispy.

Remove with a slotted spoon and drain on kitchen paper.

Wash and roughly chop the tomatoes.

Put the bread cubes into a bowl.

Add the tomatoes, onion, lemon juice, coarse sea salt, plenty of freshly ground black pepper, and the basil.

Toss well and serve.

Rich in vitamin A and natural sulphur for maximum immunity

Back to the roots

Root vegetables are sadly ignored in many homes today – more's the pity. They are cheap, easy to use, and a powerhouse of immune-enhancing nutrients.

Old carrots are super-rich in betacarotene, which your body converts into vitamin A, a vital part of the natural defence mechanism. Turnips, another member of the cabbage family, contain the sulphurous compound raphanol, which is antibacterial; as a bonus, turnips are good for gout, too. Celeriac is a major source of the phytochemical apigenin, which is protective against many types of cancer. All in all, this is a great immune-boosting salad with an interesting texture and flavour.

2 large old carrots

Half a medium celeriac

2 small turnips

6 radishes

4 spring onions

1 handful of fresh parsley

3 tablespoons standard salad dressing (*see* page 7)

Wash, scrape, and grate the carrots into a bowl.

Peel and grate the celeriac into a separate bowl.

Thinly slice the peeled turnips.

Wash and thinly slice the radishes.

Wash, trim, and finely slice the spring onions lengthways.

Wash and chop the parsley.

Mix some of the dressing with the carrot and celeriac. Press each into two timbale pots (or small jelly moulds) and chill for half an hour.

Turn out onto a large plate and decorate with spring onions and radish and turnip slices.

Sprinkle with the parsley and drizzle with the remaining dressing.

A traditional healing salad with a yoghurt twist

Caraway coleslaw

Here's a combination of all the traditional healing powers of cabbage, paired with the digestive benefits of caraway seeds. All cabbages are rich sources of vitamin C and sulphur, a protective and antibacterial combination, and red cabbage contains large amounts of betacarotene. The addition of live yoghurt means a massive injection of beneficial bacteria, which play a vital role in natural immunity.

Half a small red cabbage

Half a small white cabbage

1 large dessert apple

1 handful of seedless raisins

1 small carton (150g OR 5½oz) live natural yoghurt

Juice and zest of 1 unwaxed lemon

1 teaspoon caraway seeds

Freshly ground black pepper

Wash and finely shred both cabbages.

Wash and coarsely grate the unpeeled apple.

Mix the cabbage with the apple and add the raisins.

Combine the yoghurt, lemon juice, and zest.
Mix into the cabbage mixture and stir thoroughly.

Sprinkle caraway seeds on top, and season with black pepper.

A versatile dish to ward off a variety of ills

Hot or cold Italian bake

This combination of tomatoes, courgettes, oregano, and Emmental cheese is equally delicious as a hot supper dish or served warm or cold as a salad to accompany a jacket potato, cold chicken, or cold roast beef or lamb.

It's immensely rich in lycopene, one of the carotenoid family of natural chemicals that protect against heart disease and prostate cancer. Oregano, the essential Italian herb for all tomato recipes, is full of antibacterial volatile oils which help ward off coughs, colds, and other infections. Finally, the cheese contains valuable protein and masses of calcium.

1 medium onion

2 cloves of garlic

4 medium fresh tomatoes

4 courgettes

2 tablespoons extra-virgin olive oil

1 large can (400g OR 14oz) chopped tomatoes

2 teaspoons fresh oregano leaves

Freshly ground black pepper

85g OR 3oz grated Emmental cheese

Peel and finely chop the onion and garlic.

Wash and thinly slice the fresh tomatoes and courgettes (this works just as well with thin slices of peeled marrow.)

Gently heat the oil, then add the onion and garlic and sweat until soft but not brown.

Add the chopped canned tomatoes and stir until warmed through.

Tip the contents of the pan into an ovenproof dish and add a layer of courgettes, a layer of tomatoes, a sprinkle of oregano, and black pepper, and repeat until you've used all the tomatoes and courgettes.

Cover with grated cheese and bake in a medium oven (180°C OR 350°F OR gas mark 4) for thirty minutes.

A delicious and defensive year-round, fruity cocktail

Blueberry booster

This recipe is mega-health insurance on a plate. The amazing antioxidant protection in blueberries plus the healing enzyme bromelain from pineapple and the betacarotene, vitamin E, together with the vast amount of vitamin C in the kiwi fruit all add up to a fantastic immune-boosting cocktail.

In addition, the beneficial bacteria in live yoghurt are known to play a vital role in the body's defences against infection. Winter or summer, this is a fruit salad that will help you avoid coughs, colds, and flu. It's especially good for children and teachers, who are constantly exposed to all sorts of bugs at school.

1 ripe pineapple

150g OR 5½oz blueberries

4 kiwi fruit

6 fresh mint leaves

2 small cartons (300g OR 10½oz) live natural yoghurt

1 tablespoon runny honey

Zest of half an unwaxed lemon

Peel, core, and slice the pineapple.

Wash and dry the blueberries.

Peel and slice the kiwi fruit into thin slices.

Chop the mint and stir into the yoghurt, along with the honey and lemon zest.

Arrange the pineapple slices on a large platter and fill the centre of each with blueberries.

Surround with the kiwi fruit slices and pour the yoghurt dressing on top.

ng Salads

"Detox" may be the current buzzword in natural-health circles, but it's only a pseudoscientific way of saying "cleansing". No matter how Draconian some detox diets may appear, they do seem to be growing in popularity. The reason? Well, there's no doubt that, used sensibly and occasionally, they can be valuable in terms of promoting and sustaining good health.

Unfortunately, however, many people (especially women) use such regimes as a route to instant weight loss. When detox diets help their users shed pounds, there is an enormous temptation to carry on for another week – or two, or six – until they become such a habit that a return to normal eating is virtually impossible. This path to eating disorders is one to be avoided at all costs, and anyone contemplating a serious detox regime should do so only under the guidance of a qualified and registered naturopath. Make sure that the practitioner you choose has the letters "MRN" after his or her name; this indicates a member of the General Council and Register of Naturopaths, and means that the individual has passed four years of training at the British College of Naturopathy and Osteopathy.

In much the same way as the chemical cocktail in our food, water, environment, and homes affects the body's immune system, it can also trigger allergies, food sensitivities, and a whole host of other health problems. The salads in this chapter work to counteract these problems by helping to improve the way your body eliminates the waste substances that are by-products of natural processes. They also improve the body's ability to remove other pollutants. You'll find some salad mixtures here which may look unusual, but I promise you that, as well as tasting fantastic, they all have particular properties that will help cleanse the system.

In the following pages you'll discover salads made with dandelion leaves, which are a gentle diuretic, as well as others made with radishes, which stimulate the liver. Fennel is also featured because it's another liver-stimulant that improves the digestion of fat and speeds up the rate at which the body gets rid of cholesterol. Celery and celery seeds are included for their powerful cleansing properties, beetroot is added for the blood, and watercress shows up to protect the lungs.

In addition, apples make an appearance in this chapter, because they really do keep the doctor away. They do so for many reasons, but one of their main benefits is their high content of the soluble fibre known as pectin, which not only helps lower cholesterol, but also improves the digestive function and helps keep bowels functioning regularly.

Dry, blotchy skin, spots and pimples, recurrent headaches, bloating, constipation, wind, sluggishness, or just feeling constantly several degrees under par may all be good reasons for thinking that your system needs a clean-out. Yet if you're sensible about your eating and avoid a constant diet of junk food, excessive alcohol, living out of the frying pan, and neglecting fruit and vegetables, you won't need a drastic detox regime.

Instead, to keep all systems in good working order and to avoid a build-up of waste products in the body, all you need to do is make sure you eat one of these cleansing salads two or three times a week. You'll certainly look better – and the bonus is that you'll feel better, too.

A tasty source of natural fibre

Granny's cleanser

It's hardly surprising that a lot of old wives' tales turn out to be true. After all, many of them refer to practices that have been in use for hundreds of years, and if they didn't work at all, they wouldn't stand the test of time.

    This recipe combines the traditional cleansing properties of apples with the gentle diuretic effect of celery and the high-fibre content of raisins. Add the natural bacteria in live yoghurt and you've got a salad that is not only rich in iron, vitamin C, pectin, potassium, and cleansing essential oils, but is also deliciously crunchy and bursting with flavour.

2 large Granny Smith apples, unpeeled

Juice of 1 lemon

2 sticks of celery, preferably with leaves

2 tablespoons seedless raisins

1 small carton (150g OR 5½oz) live natural yoghurt

1 tablespoon cider vinegar

3 tablespoons extra-virgin olive oil

1 teaspoon runny honey

Wash the apples and cut into small wedges. Put them into a salad bowl, add half the lemon juice, and mix thoroughly to prevent browning.

Scrub and slice the celery into 1cm OR half-inch chunks, chop the leaves, and add to the apple pieces.

Add the raisins.

Mix together the yoghurt, vinegar, oil, honey, and remaining lemon juice.

Add to the salad and toss lightly.

Rich in iron – and effective for fluid loss

Dandelion delight

In the north of England, the country name for dandelion is "wet-the-bed", and in France it's called *pis en lit* – which means exactly the same thing. In most French street markets you can buy these delicious leaves alongside all the other salad ingredients.

Although it's the root of dandelion that is the most powerful diuretic part of the plant, the leaves will also increase your water loss – hence they have a powerful cleansing action. In addition, they're rich in iron, which you'll absorb all the better thanks to the vitamin C in the lemon juice.

To maintain a local supply of this useful cleansing herb, don't poison every dandelion in your garden. And make sure you keep the dogs off them, as the delicate, pale young leaves are truly delicious and health-giving. The extra nutty flavour of the lamb's lettuce and the slight bitterness of spinach give this salad its unique flavour.

1 generous bunch of dandelion leaves	Thoroughly wash and dry all the leaves. Put them into a large salad bowl.
1 generous bunch of lamb's lettuce	Pour on the oil.
2 handfuls of baby spinach leaves	Squeeze the lemon juice over the top.
2 tablespoons extra-virgin olive oil	Toss thoroughly so that every leaf is well-coated.
Juice of half a lemon	

For efficient digestion and elimination of cholesterol

Florence fennel salad

This salad is guaranteed to help any cleansing programme, thanks largely to the natural plant chemicals provided by fennel (the bulb's "proper name" is Florence fennel). Among others, this delicious bulb contains essential oils called anethole and fenchone, which are mildly diuretic and thus help the body get rid of excess fluid. In addition, fennel is very good news for women, as its oils play an important part in maintaining hormone balance. The fibre and vitamin C in oranges, together with the red onion, improve digestive function and the elimination of cholesterol.

1 large bulb of Florence fennel

1 large red onion

2 oranges

Juice of 1 orange

2 teaspoons balsamic vinegar

A few sprigs of fresh mint, to garnish

Wash and slice the fennel as thinly as possible.

Peel and slice the onion.

Peel and slice the oranges, and put a layer of orange slices onto each of four plates.

Cover the oranges with the fennel.

Sprinkle the onion on top of the fennel.

Mix the orange juice with the vinegar and drizzle the dressing over each plate.

Garnish with the mint leaves.

A medieval tonic to spring clean digestion

Bittersweet treat

Chicory and all the curly endives are members of the same family of wonderful winter salad vegetables. They are all descendants of wild chicory, which has a long history in traditional herbalism as a cleanser and detoxifier. In medieval times, it was used as one of the most important late winter/early spring tonic plants to give the body a stimulating spring-clean.

The vitamin C from the oranges improves the absorption of iron from the chicory and watercress, which is also a great source of natural protective chemicals. This salad offers a wonderful combination of flavours, thanks to the sweetness of the orange, which offsets the bitter chicory, while the peppery bite of watercress adds the digestive stimulation you need during the sluggish winter months.

2 large oranges
2 bulbs of chicory
1 large bunch of watercress
Juice of 1 lime
1 tablespoon rapeseed oil
Freshly ground black pepper

Peel and thinly slice the oranges.

Separate, wash, and chop the chicory leaves into bite-sized pieces.

Wash the watercress – even if it's "ready washed".

Whisk the lime juice into the rapeseed oil.

Lay the orange slices on a serving plate and cover with the chicory leaves. Pile the watercress in the middle.

Drizzle with the rapeseed-oil dressing and season with pepper.

An anti-inflammatory dish with a diuretic bonus

Waterfall salad

As you'll guess from its name, this is another strongly diuretic recipe. It's great for all women who suffer uncomfortable fluid retention and swelling of ankles, fingers, and breasts around period time. This is also a valuable dish for anyone suffering with gout or arthritis, as the celery and celery seed specifically increase the elimination of uric acid, the chemical that aggravates inflamed joints.

Apples are another traditional remedy for joint diseases, and watermelon is a traditional cooling fruit that also has mild eliminative benefits.

2 sweet dessert apples

1 tablespoon raspberry vinegar

A chunk of watermelon

1 bulb of chicory

2 sticks of celery, preferably with leaves

1 teaspoon celery seed

1 tablespoon walnut oil

Wash, core, and dice the apples. Put them into a salad bowl, pour in the vinegar, and mix well to avoid browning.

Deseed the watermelon and cut into cubes.

Wash the chicory and slice into rounds.

Wash and coarsely chop the celery and celery leaves.

Add everything to the bowl of apples, along with the celery seed, and mix gently.

Pour in the walnut oil and mix again.

Stimulates cleansing organs and strengthens the blood

Red, hot, and healthy

Served on a white plate, this salad looks absolutely stunning, but it's got more than simple eye appeal. Radishes are one of the great traditional foods for stimulating the liver and gall bladder. They increase the production of bile, which in turn helps with the digestion of fat in the diet. They're also a great source of potassium, calcium, and sulphur, making this salad one good, all-round, hot little number.

Red peppers are rich in fibre, beetroot is good for the blood, and radicchio supplies some betacarotene. All in all, this is both a cleansing and immune-boosting recipe.

1 good-sized head of radicchio	Wash and separate the radicchio into individual leaves.
12 medium radishes	Wash and quarter the radishes.
2 red peppers – the dark, pointed ones if you can find them	Wash and slice the peppers into rounds and remove any seeds.
4 small cooked whole beetroot	Cut the beetroot into julienne-style strips.
1 bunch of fresh chives	Wash and finely chop the chives.
4 tablespoons standard salad dressing (*see* page 7)	Arrange the radicchio leaves in a bowl. Add the pepper slices, then the beetroot strips, then the radishes.
	Drizzle with dressing and sprinkle with the chives.

Circu

Salads

lation

Making sure that your circulation is working at optimum efficiency is literally taking care of your lifeblood. Without the heart pumping your blood to each part of the body, nothing functions as it should.

Brain, lungs, liver, kidneys, muscles, nerves, skin, and every single cell must have access to the oxygen, vitamins, minerals, and other essential nutrients that are transported by your circulating blood. Unfortunately, however, many factors can interfere with your circulation, restrict the passage of the blood, and result in problems. Most people think circulatory problems are about chilblains, varicose veins, and cold hands and feet. And, indeed, these are common symptoms, but the related difficulties can be much more complex, resulting in vertigo, headaches, high blood pressure, heart disease, haemmorrhoids, leg ulcers, skin problems, "bad hair days"… even short-term memory-loss.

To keep your circulation in good order, you need to take care of the quality of the blood, the efficiency of the heart, the health of the major arteries, and the condition of the capillaries; the latter are the tiniest blood vessels at the very end of the circulatory system. Exercise is one of the most effective ways of stimulating your heart and circulation, and any activity that increases the heart and breathing rate making you sweat is good. Three ten-minute bursts of active housework, half an hour of vigorous gardening, or a brisk walk for twenty minutes three times a week is enough. Activities such as these will all get the blood whizzing round your system, carrying its essential nutrients to every vital organ and each individual cell throughout your body.

Yet, good as it is, exercise alone is not enough. You also need to eat a good dose of the foods that are necessary to protect and nourish your heart and blood vessels – lots of which you'll find in this chapter's delicious recipes. Vitamin C from oranges, grapes, and lettuce; essential oils from fresh salmon; powerful, protective antioxidants from the natural chemicals that colour beetroot and fresh figs…all of these foods have an important part to play in any good circulation diet.

In these salads you'll also find plenty of iron in figs and dates, essential for maintaining healthy blood. Then there are substances that stimulate the circulation; these are found in rocket, radishes, and chillies. The amazing natural cleansers contained in garlic, onions, and chives help the body get rid of artery-clogging cholesterol. Vitamin E is another essential nutrient for good circulation, and is found in abundance in the extra-virgin olive oil and walnut oil used in the salad dressings. The betacarotenes in all red, yellow, and orange fruits and vegetables are the final ingredients that help nourish and maintain the integrity of your heart and blood vessels – which is why they are used here in quantity.

It's all too easy to associate poor circulation with wintertime, and cold weather is certainly not the "natural" season to think of eating salads. Hot soups, hearty stews, and plenty of stodge are the more traditional forms of comfort eating when the weather turns nasty, yet they're not always the best solution. Whatever the temperature, remember that these circulation salads will come to your rescue if you're having problems. Of course, the best idea is not to wait until things go wrong. By adding circulation salads to your regular diet now, you'll discover an enjoyable way of protecting yourself against any future problems – and you'll feel better into the bargain.

Helps regulate hormones and boost sluggish blood

Fennel, rocket, and radish salad

The familiar flavour of fennel used as a herb is found in many fish dishes, but this salad uses the large white bulb of the Florence fennel. Its crunchy texture and unusual flavour of mild liquorice is beautifully complemented by the sharp bite of rocket and radishes.

Fennel contains natural chemicals, including anethole and fenchone, and has the specific effect of helping to regulate hormonal imbalances. This makes it an invaluable plant for all women. Together with the circulatory stimulus of the essential mustard oils in radishes, as well as the tannins and other volatile oils in the rocket, the combination will give a quick boost to even the most sluggish of circulations.

By the way, you may think rocket is a modern phenomenon of big-city superchefs, but it was widely grown and used as both food and medicine as early as the reign of Elizabeth I.

1 large bulb of Florence fennel

12 radishes

1 generous bunch of rocket

3 tablespoons standard salad dressing (*see* page 7)

Wash and slice the fennel into rounds, saving some of the green fronds, if any. Dry the fronds.

Wash, trim, and quarter the radishes.

Wash and thoroughly dry the rocket.

Put all the ingredients, except the fronds, into a salad bowl. Add the dressing and toss lightly.

Sprinkle any fennel fronds over the top.

A circulatory stimulant and energy building combination

Citrus fig salad

Since the time of ancient Greece, figs have been renowned for their restorative and energy-building properties. They were so highly prized that the earliest Olympic athletes were fed pounds of them to improve their performance – with good reason. Figs are full of blood-building nutrients, and they contain the natural enzyme ficin, which improves the digestive absorption of the fruit's other constituents, especially the iron that is so vital for healthy blood and circulation.

The added benefits of essential oils in tarragon and the generous amounts of vitamin C in the lemon juice are what make this salad a circulatory stimulant.

8 ripe figs

1 generous bunch of lamb's lettuce

2 tablespoons coarsely chopped fresh tarragon leaves

Juice of 1 lemon

1 tablespoon extra-virgin olive oil

Wash, dry, and quarter the figs.

Wash and dry the lamb's lettuce.

Put the lamb's lettuce into a serving bowl with the tarragon.

Thoroughly mix the lemon juice with the olive oil.
Add to the bowl and toss thoroughly to coat all the surfaces.

Arrange the figs over the top.

A light but effective blood-builder

Beetroot and orange with chives

Throughout Eastern Europe, beetroot has been a traditional remedy for blood and circulatory disorders for centuries; in fact, the juice is given to anyone suffering from leukaemia. Combined here with slices of fresh orange, rich in protective vitamin C and bioflavonoids, and the heart and circulatory benefits of chives, this is a light, delicious, and appealing dish.

3 large cooked whole beetroot

2 large oranges

1 bunch of fresh chives

6 chive flowers (optional)

3 tablespoons standard salad dressing (*see* page 7)

Peel the beetroot and cut into thickish slices.

Peel the oranges, remove as much pith as you can, and slice into thin rounds.

Wash and dry the chives and chive flowers.

Arrange alternate slices of beetroot and orange on one large platter or four individual plates.

Scatter the whole chives over the top.

Decorate with the chive flowers, if desired; they are edible and taste delicious.

Drizzle with the dressing and serve.

Heart-protective and packed with antioxidants

Shades of salmon red

With a slice of good, crusty wholemeal bread, this salad makes a meal for four. To use as a starter, reduce the quantities accordingly.

All oily fish is good for the circulation, and salmon is one of the best. Although it is more expensive, it's really worth choosing wild salmon, as it not only tastes better but will not contain the chemicals added to the feed of farmed fish. The omega-3 fatty acids in the fish protect both the heart and arteries, and help prevent the build-up of plaque inside the blood vessels.

Red peppers are one of the best sources of betacarotene and the antioxidant vitamin C, both of which provide further protection. The capsaicin in the green chillies stimulates blood flow by dilating the circulatory system's tiny capillaries.

As a final boost, you get all the benefits of garlic and the bonus of extra calcium from the yoghurt.

675g OR 1½lbs fresh wild salmon	Put the salmon into a large pan of cold water with the bay leaves, peppercorns, and dill. Bring slowly to the boil, turn off the heat, and leave to cool.
2 bay leaves	
6 peppercorns	
1 sprig of fresh dill	Remove the skin from the fish and flake into a bowl.
1 large red pepper	Wash, deseed, and chop the pepper into small cubes.
1 small fresh green chilli	Wash, deseed, and slice the chilli very thinly.
1 clove of garlic	Peel and chop the garlic.
7.5cm OR 3-inch chunk of cucumber	Peel and chop the cucumber.
1 small carton (150g OR 5½oz) live low-fat natural yoghurt	Stir the garlic, chilli, and cucumber into the yoghurt, pour over the flaked salmon, and stir gently.
1 head of radicchio	Wash, dry, and separate the radicchio leaves. Arrange the salad on top and serve.

A rich source of vitamin E for a healthy heart and circulatory system

Nutty dates and grapes

An unusual mixture of bean sprouts from the culinary traditions of the Far East, almonds and dates from the Middle East, and grapes from southern Europe make this a super circulation booster.

Bean sprouts are rich in vitamin E, an essential nutrient for a healthy heart and circulation. Dates are an excellent source of iron, the blood-building mineral that is frequently lacking in modern diets. Almonds provide essential fatty acids and protein, while the grapes contain abundant amounts of circulation-protecting antioxidants, as well as vitamin C.

1 bag of bean sprouts

20 seedless black and white grapes

12 fresh dates

1 tablespoon walnut oil

1 teaspoon sesame oil

1 teaspoon balsamic vinegar

1 teaspoon light soy sauce

2 tablespoons blanched almond halves

Freshly ground black pepper

Thoroughly wash and dry the bean sprouts.

Wash and halve the grapes.

Halve the dates and remove the stones.

Arrange the salad in four serving bowls, putting the bean sprouts in the bottom and sprinkling the other ingredients on top.

Whisk together the oils, vinegar, and soy sauce.

Drizzle each bowl with a little dressing – but don't toss.

Scatter over the almonds and season with black pepper.

Skin-cl

Salads

eansing

Few people realize that the skin is the largest organ of the body, but most know that the psychological importance of its appearance is incalculable. You present your skin to the outside world. If it's blotchy, flaky, covered in pimples, acne, or sore patches, it undermines your confidence and affects the way you relate to others.

Your skin is more than just a protective covering. Like your kidneys, bowels, and lungs, it helps to detox the system by getting rid of metabolic waste products. The old adage "you are what you eat" applies more to healthy skin than almost any other part of your body. Anyone who suffers from eczema will almost certainly have discovered that there are foods that help and foods that aggravate this skin condition. It doesn't matter what you do to the outside of your skin; it's what you put *into* the body that can make a difference. No amount of expensive cosmetics, exfoliants, cleansers, moisturizers, face masks, or prescription lotions and potions will make up for a diet of junk food that is high in saturated fat, salt, sugar, and chemical additives.

The eyes may be the window of the soul, but your skin is a reflection of your general health, and its condition is quickly affected by nutritional deficiencies. Three key substances are important to the maintenance of healthy, vital, and glowing skin: vitamins A and C, and the mineral zinc. That's why the salads in this chapter provide significant amounts of these nutrients, with the additional benefits of vitamin E, betacarotene, and natural gentle diuretics that increase the efficiency of your eliminative functions.

Mediterranean vegetables such as aubergines, peppers, and fennel are major sources of betacarotenes. Tomatoes provide vitamin C and the important nutrient lycopene, which is not only good for your skin, but protective against heart disease and breast and prostate cancers. Vitamin E is another important skin nutrient that prevents ageing, wrinkling, and stretch marks, which is why avocado is such an important ingredient here. Sadly, many women regard this delicious fruit as fattening because it's oily, but it should be every woman's best friend in terms of skin health and complexion. Prawns and pumpkin seeds are rich sources of zinc, and watercress, oranges, apples, spinach, and lemon juice provide more of the essential vitamin C and bioflavonoids.

Whatever your particular skin problems, these salads will help, since they are rich in foods providing vital nourishment for vital skin. In addition, they also encourage the other organs of elimination to work more efficiently; this, in turn, reduces the amount of irritant substances excreted through the skin and also speeds up the healing of damaged areas.

A word of advice, however: using food as medicine doesn't produce results overnight, and this is particularly true with skin problems. It may take several weeks of adding these salads to your regular meal plan, but persevere and you will see dramatic improvements. Just remember that one of the great pioneers of the cosmetics industry, Helena Rubenstein, had a favourite saying: "Don't put anything on your face that you wouldn't put in your mouth." How right she was. If you've got skin problems, there is no point in adding these beneficial salads to your diet if the rest of it is made up of burgers, chips, takeaways, chocolate, biscuits, and regular helpings of Black Forest gateaux.

Protects against break-outs with plenty of zinc and sulphur

Fresh, green, and clean

Everyone will enjoy this unusual but simple combination, but for those suffering the agonies of acne, it's a must and should be eaten once or twice a week.

Watercress is a much-maligned plant, usually relegated to a garnish on top of the steak and nearly always left on the side of the plate. What a tragic waste! Watercress is rich in sulphur compounds, natural antibiotics that help to prevent and get rid of those unsightly acne spots. It also contains iron, iodine to stimulate the thyroid gland, and unique natural chemicals that protect against lung cancer. Rich in vitamins A and C, every leaf helps improve your skin.

The plus points in this salad are the pumpkin seeds. As one of the richest vegetable sources of zinc, they add more skin-healing properties to the dish. Zinc is a mineral often deficient in modern convenience foods. Not only is it essential for the structure and elasticity of skin, but a lack of zinc is one of the prime causes of chronic fatigue.

1 large bunch of watercress

2 oranges

2 tablespoons pumpkin seeds

Juice of 1 lime

Thoroughly wash and dry the watercress – even if it says it's "ready washed".

Peel and thinly slice the oranges.

Place a mound of watercress in the middle of a serving plate, and surround it with slices of orange.

Scatter the pumpkin seeds over everything.

Sprinkle with the lime juice, and serve.

A betacarotene boost for the skin and eyes

Night sight

Thanks to this salad, at least you'll be able to see your spots in the dark. If you eat enough of it, however, your skin will soon start to improve. The most important substance in carrots is betacarotene, and you can get more than a day's dose in just one large carrot. But you need to use "old" rather than newer, smaller carrots, as they're far richer in this skin-essential nutrient. Carrots are also rich in fibre; added to the unique soluble fibre known as pectin in apples, this is one salad that will benefit your skin directly and indirectly. It improves the digestive function, helping the body to eliminate waste products more efficiently.

As well as boosting natural immunity and protection from infection, the calcium and beneficial bacteria in the yoghurt are good for the bones.

3 large carrots

2 large sweet dessert apples

Juice of 1 lemon

1 tablespoon seedless raisins

1 tablespoon extra-virgin olive oil

2 teaspoons cider vinegar

1 small carton (150g OR 5½oz) live low-fat natural yoghurt

Wash the carrots; if not organic, top, tail, and peel. Cut or process into julienne strips.

Wash the apples and leave the skin on. Grate into a bowl and add the lemon juice to prevent browning.

Mix together the carrot and apple, then stir in the raisins.

Add the olive oil and cider vinegar to the yoghurt, then mix thoroughly with the salad.

Perfect source for vitamin A and other anti-ageing nutrients

Skin cooler

Like all icebergs, iceberg lettuce has hidden depths – and it's the bits you can't see that are so good for your skin. The darker, outside leaves in particular are a good source of betacarotene, which the body converts to vitamin A, an essential skin nutrient. Yet the betacarotene itself is also one of nature's skin-protectors, as its antioxidant activity destroys the free-radical chemicals responsible for ageing.

Cooked prawns not only taste great but are a good source of zinc and other skin-friendly minerals. When put together with the vitamin E-rich avocado and the lycopene in the tomatoes, this is the perfect recipe for every skin problem.

2 ripe avocados

16 ripe vine tomatoes

1 iceberg lettuce

1 generous bunch of fresh dill

450g OR 1lb cooked peeled prawns

Freshly ground black pepper

3 tablespoons standard salad dressing (*see* page 7)

Peel the avocados, halve, and cut into chunks.

Wash and cut the tomatoes roughly into chunks.

Separate the iceberg lettuce, break into pieces, then wash and dry.

Wash and dry the dill.

Arrange the lettuce into the bottom of a bowl, then add the prawns.

Scatter the chunks of avocado and tomato halves on top, sprinkle with pepper and dill, pour on the dressing, and serve.

A good source of protein and all-important B vitamins

Desert delight

This traditional lentil salad comes from the desert lands of the Middle East and North Africa. The ultimate in skin nutrition, lentils are also abundantly rich in protein: 100g OR 3.5oz will provide about two-thirds of the daily protein needs for an active man. They're also an extremely good source of iron, and contain valuable amounts of B vitamins, a lack of which will soon show up in your skin.

The vitamin C in the coriander, parsley, and lemon juice improves the absorption of iron, and the gently diuretic action of parsley will make sure that your body is getting rid of unwanted waste products through the kidneys.

280g OR 10oz green lentils

1 generous bunch of fresh coriander

1 generous bunch of fresh parsley

2 cloves of garlic

Juice of 1 lemon

1 tablespoon walnut oil

Freshly ground black pepper

Thoroughly wash the lentils, cover with water, and boil gently until tender, about twenty to thirty minutes, stirring occasionally. Make sure they don't dry out.

Strain the lentils and pour into a salad bowl.

Wash and finely chop the coriander and parsley and add to the lentils.

Finely chop the garlic and combine with the lemon juice and walnut oil.

Pour the mixture onto the lentils, mix thoroughly, and serve while still warm with plenty of freshly ground black pepper.

Provides a skin-friendly burst of betacarotene and powerful protective substances

Spinach surprise

The surprising thing about spinach is that it isn't a good source of iron. Although it does contain iron, because of the oxalic acid present in its leaves your body can't get at it. What it can get, however, is loads of betacarotene and other skin-friendly nutrients.

As well as all the heart-protective benefits of garlic, one of its most valuable traditional uses comes from its powerful antibacterial and antifungal properties. This makes it an ideal food for anyone with such problems as athlete's foot, thrush, infected spots, and other similar skin problems. Onions, too, share these properties, so this salad has a double boost of skin-friendly substances.

You might think warm vegetables sound a bit strange for a salad, but this is a popular dish in Italy, where it is often served alongside a main course of fish or meat.

1 large bag of spinach leaves

2 tablespoons extra-virgin olive oil

Juice of 1 lemon

1 clove of garlic

4 spring onions

Thoroughly wash the spinach and remove any thick stalks. Do not dry. Put into a large saucepan without adding any extra water.

Cook over a medium heat until most of the water is evaporated and the spinach has wilted.

Drain thoroughly, put into a warm dish, and drizzle with the olive oil and lemon juice.

Peel and finely chop the garlic.

Trim and coarsely chop the spring onions.

Add the spring onions and garlic to the spinach, stir thoroughly, and serve.

A barbecued batch of cleansing essential oils and phytonutrients

Slow-cooked salad

This salad is a delicious mixture of skin-friendly Mediterranean vegetables cooked on the barbecue. However, you don't have to go out into the garden when it's snowing, because this works just as well in a griddle or grill pan, or in a built-in stove-top griddle if you're lucky enough to have one.

   Masses of vitamin C and betacarotenes from the peppers, the cleansing essential oil fenchone from fennel, a generous helping of phytonutrients in the aubergine, and all the cleansing properties of onions bring a taste of Mediterranean summer to this super skin salad.

3 medium courgettes

1 large aubergine

1 large bulb of Florence fennel

1 medium red pepper

1 medium yellow pepper

1 head of broccoli

1 medium red onion

1 medium white onion

3 tablespoons extra-virgin olive oil

2 large sprigs of fresh rosemary

2 cloves of garlic, finely chopped

115g OR 4oz Manchego cheese (if you can't find it, Parmesan will do)

Wash and dry the courgettes, aubergine, fennel, and peppers.

Slice the courgettes lengthways and the aubergine crossways.

Deseed the peppers and cut them and the fennel into bite-sized chunks.

Wash the broccoli and break into florets.

Peel the onions and cut into wedges.

Heat the barbecue, grill, or griddle pan.

Lightly brush all the vegetables with the olive oil. Place on the heat, and do not touch them: they won't stick unless you move them about.

Cut the rosemary into 5cm OR 2-inch lengths and put on top of the vegetables.

Turn the vegetables when ready – about three to four minutes.

While the vegetables are cooking, put the garlic into a small frying pan with a little olive oil and cook gently until crisp and slightly golden. Do not overheat, as it will burn and taste bitter. When done, drain on kitchen paper.

When all the vegetables are slightly charred on the outside and tender in the middle, serve sprinkled with the garlic and wafer-thin shavings of cheese.

Resto

Salads

rative

We all need a bit of restorative therapy from time to time, as so many situations result in a running down of the body's driving force. When your energy evaporates, your vitality vanishes and your immune system seems to have given up the ghost. This is the perfect time to enjoy the restorative salads listed in this chapter.

Sometimes it's easy to recognize the symptoms of low reserves: at the end of a long, dismal winter, for example, or after a summer of school or university exams, or when you've been through a period of extreme stress, such as moving house, getting married or divorced, facing redundancy, or coping with a bereavement. Yet what many people don't realize is how low their natural resources can sink as a result of relentless pressures at work or the difficulties of coping with the day-to-day routine of family life.

The body can do just so much for itself, but the minute the pressures ease, the immune system collapses. This is the reason migraine so often strikes first thing on a Saturday morning, or why you fall sick on the second day of your holiday.

Another common reason for low energy levels is illness. In the past, a period of restoration and recovery was an essential part of medical care after surgery, infectious disease, and serious (and even not-so-serious) illness. As modern medicine becomes ever more technological, however, the needs of the whole person are nearly always overlooked. Once the surgeon has operated, the antibiotics have killed the bugs, or the medical intervention has solved the problem, patients are left to fend for themselves.

At this time, your immune system is at its lowest ebb and your body becomes easy prey for opportunistic viruses and bacteria. The operation may have been a complete success, but it takes patients months before they're restored to full vitality.

Any of these scenarios is the right time to introduce a huge injection of the powerful, protective, and restorative antioxidants that come from strawberries, blueberries, mangoes, and carrots. Your body will also benefit from the immune-boosting natural chemicals in coriander, garlic, sage, and watercress.

The salads on the following pages provide an abundance of minerals. One of these is zinc, from pumpkin seeds, which fights fatigue, while broad beans and sun-dried tomatoes both offer vital potassium for restoring muscle and nerve responses. Sauerkraut, the traditional eastern European fermented cabbage, supplies antibacterial sulphur. This hugely valuable restorative food is often the butt of jokes because of its tendency to cause flatulence, yet because it's made by a fermentation process, it contains high levels of natural bacteria that play an important role in the restoration of the digestive flora. These intestinal "good guys", known as probiotics, are easily destroyed by antibiotics, so they need to be replaced as soon as possible. Not only are they essential for good digestion, they also play a vital role in the maintenance of the body's natural immunity and protection against infection.

When your natural defences have been compromised by stress or illness, these salads will help shorten your period of convalescence and restore you to vigorous vitality in the shortest possible time. All the recipes are delicious in their own rights, so whatever you do, don't wait until you're ill or recovering from sickness to try them; enjoy them while you're fit and healthy. After all, a few ounces of prevention are better than a ton of cure.

An antioxidant cocktail for a quick recovery

Strawberry fare

Restoring your immune system is the key to quick recovery after any period of excessive stress or illness – and this is just the salad to give you a kick-start. Not only is it full of vitamin C, but the natural substances that give strawberries and blueberries their colour are among the most powerful of the immune-boosting antioxidants. Add the easily absorbed protein from the cottage cheese and you have a dish that appeals to the eye as well as the taste buds.

Half a large cucumber

12 large ripe strawberries

300g OR 10½oz blueberries

1 small carton (around 150g OR 5½oz) cottage cheese

Juice of 1 lime

1 tablespoon extra-virgin olive oil

2 teaspoons balsamic vinegar

6 fresh mint leaves

Peel, deseed, and dice the cucumber.

Wash, dry, and quarter the strawberries.

Wash and dry the blueberries.

Combine the cottage cheese, lime juice, oil, and vinegar.

Wash and dry the mint.

Arrange the cucumber in a serving bowl and scatter with the strawberries and blueberries. Add a large dollop of the cottage cheese dressing and mix lightly together.

Sprinkle with mint leaves, and serve.

Helps prevent infection and increase natural resistance

Bitter green salad

If you're recovering from an illness, the last thing you need is to pick up another infection. In this salad you'll get multiple protection. Garlic's age-old tradition as an antibacterial and antifungal is now scientifically proven, while watercress is full of special mustard oils that guard against coughs and colds – it's specifically protective of lung tissue. Finally, the rich source of vitamin E found in sunflower seeds will help boost your overall resistance to infection.

1 head of frisée lettuce

1 large bunch of watercress

2 cloves of garlic

2 tablespoons sunflower seeds

3 tablespoons standard salad dressing (*see* page 7)

Separate, wash, and dry the lettuce.

Thoroughly wash and dry the watercress – even if it's "ready-washed".

Peel and finely chop the garlic cloves.

Tear the lettuce into small pieces and put into a salad bowl. Add the watercress, sunflower seeds, and garlic and mix well.

Pour on the dressing and toss lightly.

A good all-round source of vitamins and minerals

Bean-sprout booster

Sprouted beans and seeds of all types should be high on your list of favourites if you're in need of a quick burst of restoration. All sprouts are a wonderful source of vitamins and minerals – and they're cheap and easy to grow yourself if you fancy a bit of DIY therapy.

It's the enzymes, as well as other nutrients contained in seeds and sprouts, that are so important. They help boost the activity of the body's own enzyme systems, and this, in turn, enhances the body's absorption of essential substances. Adding walnuts increases the amount of B vitamins provided by this salad, as well as offering the extra benefits of essential fatty acids and protein.

1 bag of bean sprouts
1 bunch of watercress
200g OR 7oz shelled walnuts
2 spring onions
Half a ripe avocado
2 tablespoons walnut oil
1 tablespoon rice vinegar
1 teaspoon light soy sauce
Freshly ground black pepper

Wash and dry the bean sprouts and watercress thoroughly – even if they're "ready-washed". Put them into a salad bowl.

Coarsely chop the walnuts and the washed spring onions and add to the bowl.

Peel, destone, and mash the avocado, together with the walnut oil, vinegar, and soy sauce. Add the dressing to the bowl.

Toss well and season with black pepper.

Gives a gentle boost to the brain and nervous system

Chicken and mango tango

This is a special dish for me. Our friend Caroline made it for us when my wife, Sally, and I got married. Sally now makes it frequently and it's a particular favourite for friends who were at our wedding and are now so welcome in our home.

Chicken is the perfect restorative food for the brain and nervous system, as it contains B vitamins as well as protein. Like most tropical fruits, mangoes are a terrific source of betacarotenes, which are not only protective antioxidants but are also converted by the body into vitamin A, one of the essential nutrients for a healthy immune system.

1 large or two small ripe mangoes

2 sticks of celery

2 limes

4 large spring onions

150ml OR 5fl oz extra-virgin olive oil

1 large bunch of fresh coriander

1 medium-sized cooked chicken (or use the leftovers from yesterday's roast)

About 4 large leaves of iceberg lettuce

Half a cucumber

Peel the mango and remove the stone.

Scrub the celery thoroughly and roughly chop.

Juice the limes.

Trim the spring onions, leaving any succulent green tips, and roughly chop.

Put all the above ingredients into a food processor or blender. Blend or process on a moderate speed.

Add the olive oil gradually.

Wash and roughly chop half the coriander. Add to the dressing without whizzing any further.

Remove all the white meat from the chicken (use the rest to make super-immune-boosting chicken soup) and take off any skin and extra fat.

Wash the lettuce leaves, dry them, and arrange on a plate.

Peel, halve, deseed, and dice the cucumber, then sprinkle the pieces over the lettuce.

Pile the chicken on top and pour on the dressing. Garnish with the rest of the coriander leaves.

Restores digestive balance and increases nutritional uptake

Sauerkraut and caraway salad

It's a great shame that sauerkraut has never become as popular in Britain as it has in the rest of Europe, where most countries have a traditional recipe for this health-giving dish.

Long before freezing, shredded cabbage was preserved with salt and fermentation to provide a valuable source of vitamin C during the winter months. The beneficial bacteria that live in the digestive system are encouraged by the lactic acid formed during fermentation, and this increases the amount of nutrients absorbed by the body.

Adding carrots provides a huge boost of betacarotene, while the caraway seeds aid the digestion of sauerkraut and counteract its well-known flatulence factor.

500g OR 1lb 2oz sauerkraut

2 teaspoons caraway seeds

2 large old carrots

2 tablespoons safflower oil

1 tablespoon cider vinegar

1 tablespoon chopped fresh parsley

Drain the sauerkraut.

Mix in the caraway seeds.

Wash, peel, and finely grate the carrots; if they're organic, you need only scrub rather than peel them.

Mix together the oil and vinegar and add to the carrots.

Put the carrots into the middle of a serving dish, arrange the sauerkraut around the outside, and sprinkle with the parsley.

A bundle of nutrients for a natural lift

Broad bean, tomato, and sage

Throughout the Mediterranean, broad beans are known as fava beans, and many imaginative recipes use them fresh, raw, cooked, and dried to provide a huge source of nature's nutrients.

As well as fibre, they're rich in protein, contain no fat, offer loads of potassium, and they're a good source of selenium, zinc, and iron. In this dish, you'll get the added restorative boost from the mind-improving volatile oils in sage, together with a massive intake of lycopene from the sun-dried tomatoes.

400g or **14oz shelled broad (fava) beans, fresh or frozen**

10 sun-dried tomatoes

10 fresh purple sage leaves

1 handful of sage flowers (optional)

2 tablespoons pumpkin seeds

3 tablespoons standard salad dressing (*see* page 7)

Cook the beans in unsalted water until just tender. Plunge them into ice-water to cool and freshen.

Chop the sun-dried tomatoes coarsely.

Wash and dry the sage and tear into small pieces.

Mix together all the above ingredients in a shallow dish.

If you're lucky enough to grow your own sage, sprinkle the flowers on top.

Add the pumpkin seeds.

Add the dressing and leave to marinate for at least one hour before serving.

ular
Salads

Many years ago, one of my patients, an ex-oarsman himself, was appointed coach of the Oxford rowing team. With the intervarsity boat race just a few months away, he asked me, as a naturopath, if I knew of any way of changing the crew's diet that would improve their performance in the competition.

In those days, all athletes who needed muscle power for their sport were fed vast amounts of red meat, red meat, and more red meat. When I explained that the naturopath's approach to sport nutrition was to reduce protein consumption (and the high levels of fat that went with it), while dramatically increasing the amount of starchy foods in the diet, he was, to put it in modern parlance, gob-smacked.

In spite of considerable opposition, the coach did change the Oxford team's diet. They won that year – and for several years thereafter. Today, all athletes are encouraged to eat masses of bread, pasta, rice, potatoes, and beans, and much less animal protein. The muscle-building salads in this chapter provide a good selection of both.

Thanks to the "Popeye" cartoons, the connection between spinach and bulging muscles is indelibly etched into just about everyone's brain. Popeye was right about the spinach – but wrong about the reasons. Although it does contain a large amount of iron, spinach also has in it a chemical called oxalic acid, which combines with the iron to form an insoluble salt that the body can't absorb. However, spinach is one of the richest sources of carotenoids, and, as well as betacarotene, it contains the lesser known but equally important carotenoid known as lutein. Of course, you do need an adequate supply of protein to build strong muscles; if you're a meat-eater, then organic lamb is the ideal choice. Lamb in general is one of the few farm animals that still lives most of its life outside. In addition, thanks to the exercise they get, sheep generally have a lower fat content than intensively reared beef or pork. Choosing organic also means that you don't get all the unwanted toxic chemicals or the high fat concentrations in lean meat portions that are the result of high-protein intensive feeding. With an organic lamb chop, the fat you get is the fat you see – and that can be easily removed.

Eggs are another source of protein – in fact, they're the best source of easily absorbed protein. Unfortunately, they've had a bad press in recent years. Because egg yolks contain cholesterol, they've been on every nutritionist's hit-list of foods to avoid. The truth is that the body manufactures its own cholesterol from the saturated fat taken in through the diet; unless you already have a very high blood cholesterol level, cholesterol naturally present in eggs and shellfish isn't stored by the body. Organic free-range eggs taste good and do you good, so enjoy them – without the guilt.

Pasta and beans are key foods to remember if you're exercising and trying to build strong muscles. It's one of the great myths of our time that these complex carbohydrates (also bread, rice, and potatoes) are fattening. They aren't. In fact, they're every would-be weight-loser's friend, as they provide lots of energy and they're filling. The only reason they have a bad reputation is because of what people *do* to them – smother pasta in creamy sauces, eat potatoes as chips, and spread bread with lots of butter, then you've only yourself to blame when the scales edge upwards. Eat them as served in these salads, and you'll be putting more power in your muscles – not fat on your hips.

A protein-rich treat for after the workout

A breakfast salad

It's Sunday morning. You've just come back from your workout and you deserve this muscle-building treat. Although it's rich in muscular protein, this isn't the healthiest salad of all time – but it tastes great. Yes, there is some fat in it, but "low-fat" doesn't have to mean "no fat". Eat this brunch dish with some good wholemeal toast and a glass of fresh orange juice, and its good points more than outweigh the bad.

1 large pack of baby spinach leaves

8 rashers of lean organic back bacon

4 free-range organic eggs

Wash and dry the spinach. Spread the leaves over four plates.

Fry the bacon until crisp.

Meanwhile, poach the eggs.

When the bacon is crisp, break it into bite-sized pieces and sprinkle over the spinach.

Add the poached eggs, and trickle any remaining fat in the bacon pan over each plate.

For quality carbohydrates as well as good heart protection

Chinese spicy bean salad

All of the legumes, beans, and peas are great muscle-builders. They're rich sources of protein, B vitamins, minerals, carbohydrates, and fibre. Lots of people worry about the gas-causing problems associated with these particular foods, but the more you eat them, the more your digestive system adapts to them, and the fewer problems you'll have. In this delicious oriental salad, the addition of garlic, ginger, and a hint of cinnamon helps offset the side effects of the beans.

There is an added bonus in this dish: its special type of soluble fibre helps the body eliminate cholesterol, so this is a great heart-protector of a salad, too.

1 large can (400g OR 14oz) kidney beans

1 small can (300g OR 10½oz) borlotti beans

4 tablespoons Chinese plum sauce (available at most supermarkets)

2 pinches of ground cinnamon

1 teaspoon chopped fresh red chilli

1 clove of garlic, peeled and finely chopped

1 teaspoon grated fresh root ginger

1 small red onion

4 spring onions

2 teaspoons chopped summer savory

Strain the beans and rinse well under running water to remove the salt.

Mix together the plum sauce, cinnamon, chilli, garlic, and ginger.

Peel and finely chop the red onion.

Wash and finely slice the spring onions lengthways.

Put the beans into a bowl. Add the sauce and red onion and mix well.

Sprinkle with savory and garnish with the sliced spring onions.

Packed with energy, protein, and vitamin C

French pasta salad

The Italians aren't the only ones who love their pasta; it's equally at home on French tables. In fact, throughout the Mediterranean, the use of cooked vegetables in pasta salads is a regular favourite. This dish is a typical example.

There's masses of quick energy from the pasta, protein from the beans and ham, loads of vitamin C from the tomatoes as well as all their other nutrients – and everything is enhanced by the wonderful flavour of oregano.

400g OR 14oz fusilli or other short pasta

200g OR 7oz trimmed French beans (cook more for the previous day's lunch or supper and you'll have a quick midweek supper)

4 medium tomatoes

200g OR 7oz chopped ham – or use your favourite salami or spicy sausage

2 teaspoons fresh oregano leaves (or 1 teaspoon dried)

2 tablespoons extra-virgin olive oil

Freshly ground black pepper

Cook, rinse, and drain the pasta according to the packet instructions. It must be *al dente*, not mushy.

Wash and cook the beans until just tender – or use beans you've cooked for lunch or supper the day before. Cut the beans to about the same size as the pasta.

Wash and chop the tomatoes.

Mix all the above ingredients with the chopped ham, salami, or sausage, mix in the oregano, dress with the olive oil, and season with pepper.

A muscle-building meal of a salad with blood-building iron

Malaysian muscle

Although it's a salad, this wonderful rack-of-lamb dish is substantial enough to be a meal in itself. Its huge muscle and blood-building benefits come from the protein and iron in the meat. You also get the delicious flavour of peanut butter, the betacarotene in the mixed leaves, the natural plant hormones from the soy sauce, and the digestive benefits of coriander.

4 tablespoons extra-virgin olive oil

1 teaspoon turmeric

1 teaspoon ground cloves

1 rack of lamb (8 chops)

1 large bag of mixed salad leaves

2 tablespoons crunchy peanut butter

2 cloves of garlic, peeled and finely chopped

2 teaspoons soy sauce

1 teaspoon tamari

1 heaped tablespoon roughly chopped fresh coriander leaves

Heat the oven to maximum temperature.

Thoroughly mix two tablespoons of olive oil with the turmeric and cloves and rub all over the lamb. Put the lamb in a roasting dish and cook for exactly twenty minutes.

Remove from the oven, cover loosely with foil, and leave for fifteen minutes.

Wash and dry the mixed leaves.

Combine the peanut butter, garlic, soy sauce, and tamari with the remaining two tablespoons of olive oil in a food processor or blender.

Make a mound of the leaves on a large serving platter.

Separate the lamb chops and place them against the mound in a circle, with all the bones pointing upwards.

Sprinkle with the coriander leaves and serve with the sauce in a separate dish.

Bone-b

Salads

uilding

Because of today's obsessional interest in being slim, millions of women (and many men) constantly put their health at risk by following faddy and extreme diets. The way they avoid any sort of fat is nothing short of fanatical, and they reduce their calorie intake to levels which can't possibly maintain the minimum daily requirements of most essential nutrients.

Such perpetual dieters cut out all foods containing even the most remote hint of fat: dairy products, oily fish, nuts, seeds... even the fabulous avocado. As a result, their daily consumption of calcium falls way below what is adequate for healthy bones – and this is compounded by a virtual absence of vitamin D. To make matters worse, modern paranoia about danger from sunlight and fears of premature ageing mean that many such people make-up with sunscreen, long sleeves, trousers... anything to keep the sun off their skin. Of course, with an ever-growing incidence of skin cancer, nobody should be lying on sunbeds or cooking on the beach at midday. Yet some daily xposure to sunlight is vital because it triggers the body's own manufacture of vitamin D, without which the body cannot absorb calcium in order to build strong bones.

Bone-building is a vital, ongoing process throughout life, and it must be maintained in order to prevent the crippling brittle-bone disease known as osteoporosis. This silent killer, which in the UK affects one in eleven men and one in three woman, is nearly always preventable. A calcium-rich diet, plenty of vitamin D, and regular weight-bearing exercise should all be part of any bone-building plan. Although each is essential throughout every stage of life, they are even more important from the early teens to the twenties, when the body's bone-building activity is at its peak.

In spite of the fact that so many men develop osteoporosis, it is hardly ever mentioned as a man's problem. But the truth is that anyone, male or female, who has a parent with osteoporosis, is at far greater risk of contracting the disease. There are other factors which specifically relate to men, and the main one, low levels of the hormone testosterone, often remains undiagnosed and untreated. Men do not have the same dramatic hormone changes at puberty and during the menopause and they tend to develop osteoporosis rather later than women. But, nevertheless, it is still a disabling and crippling illness. Excessively high consumption of animal protein, salt, alcohol, canned fizzy drinks and smoking are all factors that predispose to osteoporosis. When combined with inadequate consumption of calcium-rich foods and a lack of vitamin D, the chances of getting this preventable condition increase dramatically.

The salads in this chapter can also play a part in keeping your bones healthy and strong. Every recipe in the following pages results in an interesting and delicious salad that overflows with the essential calcium and vitamin D that your body needs to build and maintain a strong skeleton. Whether you're eight or eighty, the nutrients in these salads will help keep you fit. Even if you already have osteoporosis, it's still not too late to improve your bones through better nutrition and gentle weight-bearing exercise. After forty years of my own experience with patients, I can assure you that this is true – regardless of what some doctors may tell you – so take heart. Start to regain some of your skeletal strength by incorporating these salads into your weekly diet. You'll be glad you did – and so will your bones.

Offers the triple-bone benefits of calcium, iron, and potassium

Chillied-out tuna

Nothing upsets me more than to see all the wonderful sprigs of parsley that get pushed to the sides of plates in restaurants. Parsley has a wonderful taste, and it's also full of bone-building nutrients, including calcium, iron, and potassium. Combine the tuna's masses of vitamin D – essential if your body's going to absorb calcium – as well as this high-protein fish's selenium and iodine, and you've got one potent bone-builder of a salad.

2 heads of chicory

1 large can (about 200g OR 7oz) tuna in sunflower oil

1 generous bunch of fresh flat-leaved parsley

2 cloves of garlic

1 small fresh green chilli

1 tablespoon extra-virgin olive oil

3 tablespoons standard salad dressing (see page 7)

Freshly ground black pepper

Separate the chicory leaves. Wash and dry them.

Drain the tuna.

Wash and coarsely chop the parsley, saving some for garnish.

Peel and finely slice the garlic.

Wash, deseed, and finely slice the chilli.

Heat the olive oil in a small frying pan. Add the garlic and half the chilli. Cook gently until slightly brown and crisp. Drain on kitchen paper.

Put the tuna into a mixing bowl. Add the chopped parsley, the rest of the chilli, and two tablespoons of dressing. Mix thoroughly.

On a large, round plate, arrange the chicory leaves and pile the tuna mixture next to them. Sprinkle the fried garlic and chilli over the tuna.

Decorate with remaining sprigs of parsley, drizzle with one tablespoon of dressing, season with black pepper – and enjoy!

A good source of calcium and essential fatty acids

Chickpea, herring, and red pepper

This salad combines the high calcium content of chickpeas and sesame seeds with the essential fatty acids of the oils, vitamin D in the herring, heart-protective and cancer-fighting lycopene from the sun-dried tomatoes, and all the general healthy benefits of onions and red peppers.

2 rollmop herrings

1 small can (300g OR 10½oz) chickpeas

1 small red pepper

1 medium red onion

1 small white onion

6 semi-dried (sunblush) tomatoes

1 tablespoon flaxseed oil

1 teaspoon sesame seeds

1 tablespoon fresh dill leaves

6 large red lettuce leaves

Drain the herrings and cut into 1cm OR half-inch strips.

Rinse and drain the chickpeas.

Wash and halve the pepper, remove the seeds, and dice.

Peel and chop the onions.

Wash and chop the tomatoes.

Mix together all the above in a bowl and pour on the oil.

Toss the salad and sprinkle with the sesame seeds and dill leaves.

Serve on a bed of washed and dried red lettuce leaves.

Offers ultimate bone protection for both sexes

Tip of the iceberg

The number of women who know they have osteoporosis represents the merest tip of the iceberg. This dreadful but preventable disease isn't called the silent killer without good reason. For one woman in three and one man in eleven in the UK, the first inkling of brittle bones is when they have a minor fall that results in a fracture. In the Far East, by contrast, this condition is comparatively rare – and the reason is believed to be due to a regular consumption of soya products, especially tofu.

This salad is not only extremely rich in calcium, it's full of bone-protective plant hormones known as phytoestrogens. These amazing natural chemicals also help reduce the other unpleasant symptoms of the menopause – which is presumably why the Japanese don't even have a word for hot flushes.

Ingredients	Method
1 tablespoon rapeseed oil	In a wok or deep frying pan, heat the rapeseed and sesame oils.
1 teaspoon sesame oil	Slice the tofu into quarter-inch strips. Add to the wok and stir-fry until light golden brown on both sides.
1 pack of tofu	
2 teaspoons sesame seeds	Add the sesame seeds and continue frying for another minute until the tofu is just crisp. Drain on kitchen paper.
1 iceberg lettuce	Finely shred, wash, and dry half the lettuce.
10 cherry tomatoes	
2 sticks of celery	Wash and halve the cherry tomatoes.
12 black olives	Wash and thickly slice the celery, chopping the leaves, if any.
2 tablespoons rice vinegar	In a large bowl, toss together the lettuce, tomatoes, celery, and olives.
2 tablespoons Japanese fish sauce	
2 teaspoons light soy sauce	Mix together the vinegar and fish and soy sauces.
	Pour over the salad and place the tofu strips on top.

A substantial salad packed with important vitamins and minerals

Hot and smoky

Here's another enjoyable way to get lots of vitamin D – essential for the absorption of calcium and building strong bones – not to mention vitamin C and betacarotene from the peppers. The delicious flavour of pine nuts also adds a large dose of potassium as well as generous amounts of iron and zinc. This is a quick and easy salad, substantial enough for lunch or a light supper.

1 large yellow pepper

Half a cucumber

150g OR 5½oz pine nuts

4 tablespoons mayonnaise

1 tablespoon horseradish sauce

4 smoked mackerel fillets

Wash, deseed, and dice the pepper.

Peel, deseed, and dice the cucumber.

Mix the pepper, cucumber, and pine nuts together in a bowl.

Combine the mayonnaise and horseradish.

Stir two tablespoons of the mayonnaise mixture into the vegetables.

Serve each mackerel fillet with a portion of the vegetable mixture and a mound of the remaining horseradish mayo on the side.

ming

Salads

The whole of the western world has become obsessed with weight. Considering the number of cases of obesity in North America and the UK, it's hardly surprising, but it's very unhealthy. Of course, being seriously overweight predisposes anyone to heart disease, high blood pressure, diabetes, breathing problems, backache, and arthritis – and that's just for starters.

Tragically, what I see in my patients is the great division between the obese who will never change, and the healthily normal whose one goal in life is to be thinner. Both these groups put their health at risk, either through inaction or overaction, neither of which is the sensible approach. Diets don't work; only long-term changes in the way you eat will make a permanent difference to what you weigh. To make matters worse, many of the popular diets are extremely bad for your health: high-protein/low-carbohydrate is a disaster, while "low-fat" seems to mean "no fat" to most women, but you need essential fatty acids in order to be healthy. The cabbage soup diet, banana diet, grapefruit diet, burger-and-chips diet are all equally bizarre. For all I know, someone has invented a doughnut diet – and that won't work either. Being ten per cent underweight reduces your life expectancy more than being ten per cent overweight, and being too thin is a serious factor in the development of osteoporosis in later life.

The only sensible way to control your weight is to balance the amount of calories you eat with the amount of calories you use, and to make sure that your daily meals are made up of as wide a variety of foods as possible. Remember: it's virtually impossible to get enough of all the essential nutrients from a diet that provides 1,500 calories or fewer a day. Eating good food and taking a bit more exercise will do the trick. Two fewer slices of bread and butter a day and twenty more minutes of brisk walking will eliminate approximately 350 calories, which equals 0.45kg or 1lb fat. That's all you have to do to lose it.

These salads are full of heart-protecting nutrients, a wide variety of foods and phytochemicals that will keep you bright and lively while you're trying to lose those few extra pounds. But don't do it unless you need to. Obsessive dieting can lead to eating disorders, a deadly problem, and frequently passed from mother to daughter.

There are two ways of measuring how sensible your weight is for your height and frame:

1. Body Mass Index calculates the relationship between height and weight. To work out your BMI, divide your weight in kilograms by your height in metres squared.

$$BMI = \frac{\textit{Weight in kilograms}}{\textit{(Height in metres)}^2}$$

Between 20 and 25 is ideal.
Between 25 and 30 is a bit overweight.
Between 30 to 40 is moderately obese.
Over 40 is grossly obese.
Under 20 is too thin.

2. You could also check your waist-to-hip ratio. Measure around the belly button, then around the largest part of the hips, then divide the waist measurement by the hip measurement.

A figure of 0.75 or less is ideal for women.
A figure of 1.0 or less is ideal for men.
As the number increases, so does your risk of heart disease.

A crunchy combination of vital nutrients

Coleslaw tricolore

This is cabbage, the king of vegetables, at its best. Known throughout Europe as the medicine of the poor, cabbage is full of antibacterial sulphur compounds as well as powerful, cancer-fighting natural chemicals. It's rich in vitamin C, too, and combined with the added carrots makes this salad a rich source of vitamin A. Both vitamins are essential nutrients for slimmers.

Half a white cabbage

Half a red cabbage

4 spring onions

2 large carrots

1 large cooking apple

2 tablespoons seedless raisins

4 tablespoons standard salad dressing (*see* page 7)

Wash and thinly shred all the cabbage.

Wash and finely chop the spring onions.

Wash and grate the carrots and apple.

Put all the above ingredients into a bowl.

Add the raisins and dressing and stir vigorously.

A healthy, filling salad that won't pile on the pounds

Crunchy vegetable salad

Members of the *Cruciferae* family, broccoli and cauliflower are, like cabbage, heart-protective and cancer-fighting. They also happen to be very low in calories, high in fibre, and extremely filling, and so are perfect as part of a good weight-control regime.

You'll get masses of vitamin C from the pepper, and more vitamin A from the carrots, while chervil, with its faint taste of aniseed, is one of the traditional herbalist's tonics and blood-purifiers, as it's rich in iron.

1 small cauliflower

2 heads of broccoli

1 large carrot

1 yellow pepper

1 generous bunch of fresh chervil

1 tablespoon cider vinegar

1 small carton (150g OR 5½oz) live low-fat natural yoghurt

Freshly ground black pepper

Wash the cauliflower and broccoli and separate into bite-sized florets.

Wash, peel, and dice the carrot.

Wash, deseed, and dice the pepper.

Wash and chop the chervil.

Mix all of these together in a serving bowl.

Stir the vinegar into the yoghurt. Stir into the salad and season with black pepper.

Full of terrific tomato taste, with plenty of health-giving vitamins

Four-tomato salad

In countries where they eat the equivalent of six tomatoes a day, they have less heart disease and less prostate cancer. This quick-and-easy salad is bursting with the tomato's protective nutrient known as lycopene, as well as with vitamin E (from the olive oil) and vitamin D (from the anchovies). All in all, it's a slimmer's salad that's also good for your circulation and bones.

2 beef tomatoes

6 plum tomatoes

12 cherry tomatoes

6 sun-dried tomatoes

4 anchovy fillets

3 tablespoons extra-virgin olive oil

1½ tablespoons balsamic vinegar

2 teaspoons fresh oregano leaves (or 1 teaspoon dried)

Wash the fresh tomatoes thoroughly. Slice the beef tomatoes. Quarter the plum tomatoes lengthways. Halve the cherry tomatoes. Coarsely chop the sun-dried tomatoes.

Lay the beef tomato slices on a large plate, add the plum and cherry tomatoes, then most of the sun-dried tomatoes.

Crush the anchovies with the rest of the sun-dried tomatoes into a paste and stir into the oil and vinegar.

Pour the dressing all over the salad and sprinkle with the oregano.

Streamlined protection on a plate

Nero's salad

As a member of the same family as onions and garlic, leeks are full of protective nutrients. They're especially good for all sorts of chest infections and sore throats, and have been used since ancient times to improve the voice; the Roman emperor Nero used to eat them every day. (Perhaps it's no accident, then, that the emblem of Wales is the leek!) Extra protein from the peas and the stimulating effect of mustard add the final touches to this dieter's delight.

8 baby leeks

450g OR 1lb peas, fresh or frozen

A sprig of fresh mint

4 tablespoons standard salad dressing – add extra mustard to taste

Freshly ground black pepper

Wash and trim the leeks and cook whole in unsalted boiling water until tender.

Cook the peas – if possible, in a steamer on top of the leeks.

Wash, dry, and chop the mint.

Drain the leeks thoroughly and leave both peas and leeks to cool a little.

While still warm, put two leeks onto each plate, surround with peas, pour on the dressing, and sprinkle with a little mint.

Season with pepper.

Warming, nutritious, and delicious

Modena salad

Modena is the home of balsamic vinegar, which gives this extremely simple salad its wonderful warm flavour. Warm vegetables are extremely popular in Italy, and the heat of the runner beans releases volatile oils from the onions and vinegar, which makes this dish smell as good as it tastes.

700g OR 1lb 9oz runner beans

1 medium onion

2 tablespoons balsamic vinegar

2 teaspoons runny honey

Coarse sea salt

Wash, trim, slice, and cook the beans in unsalted water until just tender. Drain and leave for a few moments to dry.

Peel and finely chop the onion.

Mix together the balsamic vinegar and honey.

Pile the beans into a shallow dish and add the chopped onion and a sprinkle of coarse sea salt.

Pour on the dressing.

d Salads

I've always found it difficult to understand how people can ignore the obvious links between mood and food. After all, anyone who has ever had a hangover knows how depressed you feel the next day. Similarly, almost everyone understands the mental boost you get from a cup of good, strong coffee – which is exactly the same reason a cup of tea is the universal British solution for every type of shock, trauma, or emotional upset.

Yet even if they've never made the connection, almost everyone recognizes the phrase "comfort eating", because the lack of mental energy that follows long periods without food has been experienced by all of us at one time or another. That's why that sluggish feeling makes such a wonderful excuse for a self-indulgent bar of chocolate: you get instant energy and a feel-good factor.

The good-mood salads in this chapter help to redress the two main factors that make up the link between your food and how you feel. Your brain must have a constant supply of oxygen and sugar in order to function properly; that means your blood must contain a constant amount of sugar. Unfortunately, many people fall into what I call the "sugar trap". High-sugar foods satisfy your sugar craving and give you an instant mental boost, but it's not long before this sugar is used up, as your body produces a surge of insulin to break it down – and the sugar craving comes back with a vengeance. You eat more biscuits, sweets, and chocolate; you feel great. Then, however, the cycle starts again, and you're locked into the yo-yo swing between high and low blood-sugar levels. Apart from sugar, other natural chemicals in certain foods enhance brain function, improve concentration and mental performance, and help the brain produce its own feel-good chemicals. The good-mood salads in this chapter will introduce you to the types of food that provide slow-release energy to keep your blood-sugar level on an even keel, ironing out any peaks and troughs into the bargain. They will also supply a variety of essential oils and other natural nutrients that have a direct chemical effect on your brain cells – which means that they can be mood-enhancing.

Basil, for example, has emotionally calming properties that have been understood since the time of the ancient Greeks. The complex carbohydrates in noodles, tabbouleh, and oatmeal contain an abundance of vital, slow-release energy. In addition, oily fish such as whitebait are rich sources of the amazing essential fatty acids that are vital for brain development and function.

Believe it or not, the humble lettuce is good for your brain, too. Almost all modern varieties are descended from the original wild lettuce, which the ancient Greeks used as an effective mild tranquillizer and sleep-inducing remedy. Gardeners among you will know that when you cut a lettuce, a sticky white sap oozes from the stem. The Greeks used this to prepare their sleeping draughts, because it contains morphine-like substances that are also present in tiny amounts in the lettuce leaves themselves.

That is why the Continental tradition of starting meals with a salad makes so much sense. The calming effects of the lettuce help diners relax, unwind, and enjoy their evening. You can do it, too. If you're stressed, anxious, and wound-up after a hard day, make sure you include a leafy salad in your evening meal – especially one from this particular chapter.

A calming combination that benefits the senses

Aromatherapy salad

Aromatherapy doesn't just mean a special type of massage. The benefits of this wonderful treatment come from a combination of touch and smell. This mood-boosting salad assaults your olfactory senses with the pungency of onion and the heavy, sweet scent of basil. You'll hardly have to eat it to feel better.

6 ripe organic tomatoes, the freshest and best you can buy

1 large red onion

1 generous bunch of fresh basil

4 tablespoons extra-virgin olive oil

Freshly ground black pepper

Chunks of crusty, organic wholemeal bread

Wash and thinly slice the tomatoes.

Peel and thinly slice the onion.

Wash and dry the basil.

Layer the tomato and onion in a fairly large shallow dish.

Pour on the olive oil.

Tear the basil into small pieces and sprinkle over the top.

Season with the pepper.

Serve with the bread, making sure you leave a bit left over to mop up the succulent mixture of oil and tomato juices.

A soothing salad that gently lifts the spirits and clears the mind

Good-mood green salad

With parsley, sage, rosemary, and thyme, this may sound like a song from the past, but our ancient forebears knew a thing or two about the mood-boosting benefits of these extraordinary herbs. They weren't used for flavour alone but for their medicinal properties as well. Don't forget that all medicine started in the kitchen.

The calming power of basil, the soothing effects of all types of lettuce, and the mind-clearing power of mint, combined with the memory-boosting benefits of sage, make this beautifully light salad a mental marvel.

A good selection of mixed green leaves

A handful each of fresh basil, chives, parsley, mint, sage, and thyme

2 tablespoons extra-virgin olive oil

Juice of half a lemon

Wash and thoroughly dry all the leaves. Remove the leaves from the herbs, then wash and dry.

Tear the basil into small pieces.

Snip the chives with scissors.

Chop the parsley, mint, and sage.

Mix the thyme leaves with all the other herbs.

Mix together the olive oil and lemon juice.

Add the herbs to the leaves and combine thoroughly.

Add the dressing and toss very lightly – just enough to coat the leaves.

Boosts brain function with protein and essential minerals

Protein plus

You may think that cottage cheese is the all-time cliché of every horrible slimming diet. In fact, it's rich in protein – important for brain function – and easily digested. Add it to the walnuts for more protein, minerals, and essential fats, and the celery for its cleansing action, and you couldn't find a quicker or easier mood booster.

300g OR 10½oz full-fat cottage cheese, preferably organic

Freshly ground black pepper

1 large stick of celery, preferably with leaves

10 radishes

Half a green pepper

100g OR 3½oz chopped shelled walnuts

Put the cottage cheese into a large bowl and season with black pepper.

Wash and thinly slice the celery. If it has leaves, chop them.

Wash and quarter the radishes.

Wash, deseed, and cube the green pepper.

Mix all the above ingredients together, then sprinkle the walnuts on top.

Packed with protein and energy for good concentration

Fruity duck salad

This salad is substantial enough to be a meal, and the bit of extra work involved in making it is honestly worth the effort. It looks terrific, tastes great, and is the perfect combination of brain-activating protein, slow-release energy for extended concentration, enzymes to improve digestion, and gently calming phytochemicals from the lettuce. The perfect lunch to prepare for an afternoon of mental exertion.

4 duck breasts, skin removed

300g OR 10½oz Chinese noodles

1 large ripe papaya

2 ripe kiwi fruit

1 bag of mixed salad leaves

3 tablespoons peanut, rapeseed, or safflower oil

1 tablespoon rice vinegar

1 teaspoon light soy sauce

Put a large pan of water on to boil.

Pre-heat the grill.

Bash the duck breasts gently to flatten them.

Cook under the grill for about three minutes each side, until they're just pink in the middle.

Meanwhile, put the noodles into the water.

Wash, deseed, and slice the papaya.

Peel and slice the kiwi fruit.

Wash and dry the salad leaves. Cover a serving plate with them.

Strain the noodles and toss with the oil, vinegar, and soy sauce.

Pile the noodles on top of the leaves, then arrange the duck breasts on top of the noodles. Arrange the fruit around the plate, and enjoy!

Keeps blood-sugar levels on course for a calm, assured day

Traditional tabbouleh

This staple salad comes from the Lebanon, but it's popular throughout North Africa and the Middle East – which is why it has so many variations. Every family has its own secret method of preparation, and you can vary this recipe to suit your personal tastes. The basic ingredient is bulgar wheat, sometimes known as burghul or cracked wheat.

In the Middle East, bulgar wheat is often used instead of rice, and it's made by soaking wholewheat grains in water, then putting them into a very hot oven until they crack. They have a delicious nutty flavour and are rich in protein and B vitamins. What's more, bulgar wheat is a good source of slow-release energy, which will keep your blood sugar – and your moods – on an even keel.

150g OR 5½oz bulgar wheat

2 cloves of garlic

6 tablespoons extra-virgin olive oil

Juice of 1 lemon

2 ripe plum tomatoes

Half a cucumber

4 spring onions

4 tablespoons chopped fresh flat-leaved parsley

4 tablespoons chopped fresh mint

Freshly ground black pepper

Stand the bulgar wheat in a bowl of cold water for half an hour.

Peel and finely chop the garlic, mix with the olive oil and lemon juice, and leave to marinate while you prepare the rest of the salad.

Wash and coarsely chop the tomatoes.

Peel, deseed, and chop the cucumber.

Wash and finely chop the spring onions.

Strain the bulgar wheat, getting it as dry as possible, then put into a serving bowl. Add the tomato, cucumber, spring onions, parsley, and mint.

Add the garlic dressing and stir thoroughly. Season with plenty of freshly ground black pepper.

Cover tightly with cling film. It will taste good in an hour or two but fantastic if you leave it until the next day.

A mood-booster for the brain, filled with slow-release energy

Old wives' salad

As usual, the old wives' are right as far as this tale is concerned: fish really is good for your brain. In this salad, it's even more beneficial, due to all the B vitamins and slow-release energy of oatmeal. Using chilli oil provides an enormous boost to the circulation, thanks to the capsaicin that chillies contain, so the brain is guaranteed all the blood it needs to keep it – and you – happy.

750g OR 1lb 10oz fresh whitebait
6 tablespoons fine oatmeal
1 good head of lollo rosso
Half an iceberg lettuce
Rapeseed oil, enough for frying
3 tablespoons chilli oil
1 tablespoon real malt vinegar
2 teaspoons runny honey

Wash and dry the whitebait.

Put the oatmeal into a large plastic bag.

Add the whitebait and shake vigorously until all the fish are well-coated.

Wash and dry the lollo rosso.

Shred, wash, and dry the iceberg lettuce.

Spread the lollo rosso over the bottom of a serving dish. Pile the iceberg on top.

In a deep frying pan, heat the rapeseed oil, add a handful of whitebait, and cook until crisp – approximately two to three minutes. Drain on kitchen paper. Repeat until all the fish are cooked.

Pile the whitebait on top of the lettuce.

Mix together the chilli oil, vinegar, and honey and pour over the salad.

Winter

warming
Salads

I've never understood why most people seem to think it mandatory to stop eating salads when the clocks go back in the autumn, avoiding them like the plague until the time changes again in the spring. It's as if there's a universal fear of being struck by a bolt from the blue if a single leaf of lettuce is allowed to pass your lips during any of the winter months.

Instead, winter is seen as the time for fare made up of all those traditional high-fat, high-salt, high-sugar comfort foods: steak-and-kidney pudding, bread pudding, black pudding, Lancashire hotpot, Irish stew, treacle tart, or even the now politically correct "spotted Richard". As the days get shorter, the miseries of seasonal affective disorder (SAD) or just plain winter blues are compounded by piling on the pounds. Everything slows down – and that includes mental and physical activity. As the temperature drops, the circulation slows down, too, bringing the discomfort of freezing hands and feet, the pain of chilblains, and the agonies of Raynaud's disease. The combined effects of winter winds, central heating, and office environments that are drier than the Sahara Desert cause your skin to suffer as a result of dehydration. It gets dry and flaky, unsightly blotches appear, and lips, fingers, and heels start to crack.

Yet it doesn't have to be like this. The winter-warming salads contained in this chapter will keep the blood whizzing around your veins and arteries, and ensure that your body's in-built central heating system is working at its most efficient level. The abundance of winter nutrients these salads provide will help protect your skin, maintain the quality of your blood, feed your brain, and keep your spirits up during those dark, winter days.

This isn't the time for just a few leaves of lettuce and a chopped tomato, however. What you really need are all those winter-warming spices, particularly ginger, which is rich in the essential oil known as gingerol that boosts your blood flow and "gingers up" the entire circulatory system. Don't forget chilli, either, this amazing spice helps open up the tiniest blood vessels at the very ends of the circulatory system and sets the blood coursing through your fingers and toes, raising your skin temperature and bringing a warm, comforting glow to hands and feet. The curry that brings you out in a sweat makes you feel as warm, while cayenne pepper does much the same.

It's also essential to take better care of your heart when the weather gets colder. Nowhere else in Europe does the number of older people dying of heart disease during the winter increase so dramatically as in the UK. Anyone who already has heart disease, high blood pressure, or raised cholesterol is at much greater risk when the weather gets colder. Just like the oil in your car engine, blood thickens at low temperatures, which means the heart has to work much harder to pump it around the body. If an underlying weakness is already present, this extra effort may be just enough to trigger a heart attack.

That's why you'll find lots of garlic in the following recipes. The amazing properties of this pungent bulb include the ability to thin the blood to prevent the risk of clotting, to lower cholesterol, and reduce high blood pressure. Naturally, none of these recipes will help if you're standing in sub-zero temperatures at a bus stop or on a train station without a hat, coat, and gloves, so wrap up warm – both inside and out!

Kick-start for the heart and circulation, and bursting with antioxidants

Warming pepper salad

Sweet peppers are a nutritional superstore. They're full of vitamin C, and the red, yellow, and orange varieties contain massive amounts of betacarotene. This is a multi-talented nutrient; apart from the antioxidant effect through which it protects the linings of your arteries, it's also converted by the body into vitamin A – another essential for a healthy heart and circulation.

If you can, try to avoid the perfectly shaped, supermarket-packaged peppers, most of which are grown hydroponically – that means in artificially fertilized water. Instead, look for the long, pointed, misshapen peppers that are likely to have higher levels of essential nutrients.

1 each red, yellow, and orange pepper

1 clove of garlic

1 tablespoon chilli oil

2 tablespoons extra-virgin olive oil

1 tablespoon balsamic vinegar

Half a teaspoon cayenne pepper

1 tablespoon chopped mixed fresh herbs: parsley, sage, thyme, marjoram, oregano, and chives

Wash, deseed, and dice the peppers.

Peel and finely chop the garlic. Mix thoroughly with the peppers.

Combine the oils and vinegar and whisk in the cayenne pepper. Pour over the peppers.

Mix the herbs thoroughly with the peppers.

Leave to marinate for at least thirty minutes before serving.

Stimulates blood flow; packed with wintertime nutrients

Curried bean and egg salad

Commercially produced curry powder is almost never used by real Indian cooks, as nearly every family makes its own. However it is still a wonderful winter-warmer. The spices in this salad stimulate increased blood flow, and turmeric – an essential part of any curry powder or paste – is a particularly powerful antioxidant that protects against many forms of cancer. The beans provide natural plant hormones, while the eggs are a rich source of body-building protein and winter-resistance nutrients.

4 hard-boiled eggs

300g OR 10½oz can green flageolet beans

300g OR 10½oz can borlotti beans

2 teaspoons curry powder

6 tablespoons mayonnaise

1 red onion

2 tablespoons chopped fresh coriander leaves

Shell and slice the eggs into rounds.

Drain and thoroughly rinse the beans to remove all the salt.

Whisk the curry powder into the mayonnaise and stir into the beans, mixing thoroughly.

Peel and finely slice the onion and mix into the beans.

Arrange the egg slices on top and sprinkle with the coriander.

A bundle of B vitamins to maximise the oxygen-carrying ability of blood

B-warm salad

This delicious combination of chicken livers, lettuce, grapes, and parsley is a real winter blood-builder – and good blood is the key to keeping warm in the winter. Chicken livers take minutes to cook and are an amazingly good source of protein, easily absorbed iron, and vitamin B_{12}, high levels of which are essential for the oxygen-carrying ability of blood.

Absorption of iron is increased by vitamin C from the parsley and lettuce, and you'll get wonderful heart protection from the antioxidants in the grapes.

500g OR 1lb 2oz chicken livers

1 head of Cos lettuce

20 seedless black grapes

1 generous bunch of fresh parsley

2 cloves of garlic

55g OR 2oz unsalted butter

4 tablespoons extra-virgin olive oil

Freshly ground black pepper

Wash and dry the chicken livers, removing any white membranes.

Wash, dry, and tear the lettuce into small pieces.

Wash and halve the grapes.

Wash, dry, and coarsely chop the parsley.

Peel and flatten the garlic with the blade of a large knife.

Put the butter, oil, and garlic into a large frying pan and heat gently. When hot, remove the garlic and add the chicken livers.

Turn up the heat and fry the livers for three minutes, shaking frequently to make sure they're all coated with the oil. Don't overcook – they should be slightly pink in the middle.

Put the lettuce into the bottom of a shallow dish. Add the livers, pouring over any remaining oil from the pan.

Scatter the grapes on top. Sprinkle with parsley and pepper, and serve while still warm.

A hot and healthy treat to thaw the coldest winter's day

Devil's pasta

This salad is based on the traditional Italian dish, *pasta arabiata* or *diabollo* – "devil's sauce". Make it as hot as you like, since the more chilli it has, the more warming it is (but remember that your friends have to eat it, too.) If you don't break out into a sweat after this winter-warming salad, you haven't made it hot enough. Delicious warm or cold, this is an ideal dish for the freezing months of winter.

2 sprigs of fresh parsley

1 teaspoon dried oregano

1 teaspoon chilli powder

1 pinch of cayenne pepper

2 cloves of garlic

2 teaspoons red wine vinegar

1 tablespoon extra-virgin olive oil

25g OR 1oz passata

100g OR 3½oz mange-tout

2 medium courgettes

6 medium chestnut mushrooms

200g OR 7oz baby sweetcorn

400g OR 14oz penne

3 tablespoons freshly grated Parmesan cheese

Put the parsley, oregano, chilli, cayenne pepper, garlic, vinegar, and olive oil into a food processor or blender and whiz together.

Add the passata and whiz again, briefly.

Wash and dry all the vegetables. Cut the mange-tout into 2.5cm OR 1-inch pieces. Trim and coarsely grate the courgettes. Thinly slice the mushrooms.

Put the penne into a large saucepan of boiling salted water and cook briskly, uncovered, until *al dente*.

Strain and shake off the surplus water. Return to the saucepan, add the sauce, and stir over a low heat until the pasta is well-coated and the sauce hot.

Add all the vegetables, turn into a large bowl, and eat while still warm, sprinkled with the Parmesan.

Easy and nutritious, with plenty of energy

Fresh mussels and new potatoes

For some reason, many people get nervous about cooking molluscs. Don't be. They're very quick, very easy, and very nourishing. Because of their high content of minerals and essential fatty acids, they're especially good during the winter, when they help improve the circulation. Combined here with delicious potatoes, they're an instant energy boost and a feel-good taste of luxury.

600g OR 1lb 5oz small evenly sized new potatoes

1kg OR 2lb 4oz fresh mussels in their shells

1 bunch of fresh parsley

70g OR 2½oz unsalted butter

Freshly ground black pepper

4 large spring onions, finely chopped

Put the potatoes into a large saucepan of cold, unsalted water. Bring slowly to the boil and cook until tender but not falling apart.

Thoroughly wash the mussels under running water. Pull off the beards and discard any open ones that don't close if you bang them on the table.

Put the mussels into an empty saucepan. Cover tightly and turn on the heat. You don't need any water (believe me!). After five minutes, the shells will open, releasing the sea water inside the mussels, and they're cooked.

Wash and finely chop the parsley. Add to the mussels with the butter and black pepper. Shake the pan well.

Strain the potatoes and put them into a large serving bowl. Pour on the mussels and all the sauce, then sprinkle with the spring onions.

This dish is best eaten communally, like fondue, but use your fingers instead of skewers.

Good winter protection with a bite of chilli and warming spices

Tiger, tiger

This is a bit of a luxury – but why not? It will really cheer you up in the depths of winter – or at any time of year, actually. There's lots of immune-boosting zinc from the prawns, and the warming spiciness of chilli and ginger, more winter protection from the spring onions, and lots of artery-protecting lycopene from the tomatoes. This salad makes a wonderful light lunch or a really showy starter.

Half a large cucumber

4 large firm tomatoes

1 green pepper

1 fresh red chilli

6 spring onions

2 tablespoons peanut oil

3 teaspoons sesame oil

6 thin slices of peeled fresh root ginger

2 cloves of garlic, peeled and flattened

12 large tiger prawns, cooked or fresh

1 teaspoon light soy sauce

Peel, halve, deseed, and chop the cucumber.

Wash and chop the tomatoes.

Wash, deseed, and chop the green pepper.

Wash, deseed, and chop the chilli.

Wash and slice the spring onions lengthways as finely as you can.

Mix together the cucumber and tomatoes and put into a large serving bowl.

In a large wok or deep frying pan, heat the peanut and sesame oils. Add the pepper, chilli, ginger, and garlic and stir briskly.

Add the prawns. If they're already cooked, they'll only take two minutes at maximum heat. If they're raw, they'll take a maximum of four minutes; you'll know they're done when they turn from grey to pink all over. Shake vigorously over maximum heat while cooking to make sure they're well-coated with the oil and spices. When almost done, add the soy sauce.

Arrange the prawns on top of the salad.

Remove the garlic and pour the remaining oil on top. Garnish with the spring onions.

Salads

Fertility is on the wane. Sperm counts have dropped in the last fifty years, and an ever-growing number of women are failing to conceive. Why? There are two practical reasons, with a variety of common causes.

Firstly, declining nutritional standards compromise the quality and fertility of eggs and the quantity and quality of sperm. Secondly, there appears to be a national decline in libido (at least in the UK). If you do it and one or other partner (or both) are suffering from low fertility, the chances of conception are poor. If you don't do it, then there's no chance at all. The sexy salads in this chapter will help you overcome both problems.

The modern obsession with fast food – takeaways, ready meals, instant products that require the addition of boiling water – coupled with a declining consumption of fresh fruit and vegetables has had a drastic effect on modern man's total intake of essential nutrients. Even if you try to eat more fresh produce, the vitamin and mineral content of most has fallen dramatically due to the rise of intensive farming.

The chart opposite is calculated from official UK government tables. It shows clearly that you'd have to eat twice as many carrots, apples, oranges, tomatoes, or spinach to get the same amount of minerals you'd have consumed fifty years ago. By contrast, organic produce, that has been grown in naturally fertilized soil without the use of vast amounts of toxic chemicals, still contains the same optimum levels of nutrients as it used to.

Another hazard that affects libido and fertility is the chemical cocktail of hormones that end up in dairy products, meat, and drinking water. These can all have dire consequences as far as general fertility is concerned, and are thought to be a prime

Percentage nutrient loss over fifty years

	Calcium	Iron	Potassium	Magnesium	Selenium
Broccoli	75				
Carrots	45	50	23	75	
Tomatoes	50		14	37	
Strawberries	55				
Raspberries	39				
Blackberries	35				
Spring onions	74				
Spinach		60			
Swede		70			
Watercress	23		26	12	
Apples		66			
Oranges		66	25		
Green peppers			43		
Runner beans			21	30	
Potatoes			37	29	
White flour					43
Wholemeal bread					52
Melons				45	

factor in the production of sperm counts. It's also worth noting that around half of all women attending fertility clinics have been on low-calorie slimming diets during the year before their clinic appointments. If you want to be sexy and fertile, it's important to eat enough, and even more important to eat the right nutrients. You'll find these in the salads here: root vegetables such as carrots, celeriac, and beetroots for essential minerals; rice and potatoes for that necessary energy. Eggs for iron, vitamins, and protein; plus, you'll also find traditional aphrodisiacs such as saffron, avocado, asparagus, and celery.

Whether you're trying to conceive, or just want to rekindle old flames, any of these recipes makes a perfect light meal as a prelude to a night of consuming passion.

Provides a sexy boost of vitamin E

Lover's treat

This is a salad that will bring a glint to the eye of any man or woman, as it's a true bringer of jollity and love. The avocado is a much-maligned food, but contrary to the perceived wisdom and dire warnings of ill-informed slimming gurus, it's not fattening. It is rich in vitamin E (the love vitamin for both sexes), is great for the skin, and helps the body get rid of cholesterol. The mustard oils in watercress are a sexual stimulant, and the pine nuts provide even more vitamin E and essential minerals.

2 ripe avocados

1 bunch of watercress

2 tablespoons pine nuts

3 tablespoons standard salad dressing (*see* page 7)

Halve, destone, and peel the avocados. Cut each half into thin slices.

Wash and thoroughly dry the watercress, discarding any very tough stalks. Pile the watercress into the centre of a serving plate.

Lay the slices of avocado around the watercress. Sprinkle all over with the pine nuts and drizzle with dressing.

Ultimate fertility symbol and complete energy giver

Saffron eggs

Eggs are the ultimate symbol of fertility, and in this unusual salad they provide iron, vitamins, and protein for performance. When you put them together with energy-giving potatoes, the combination is a real romantic winner. The sting in the tale is saffron, revered since ancient times as a potent aphrodisiac.

150g OR 5½oz fine French beans

500g OR 1lb 2oz new potatoes

4 spring onions

1 sprig of fresh tarragon

1 pinch of saffron

6 tablespoons mayonnaise

4 hard-boiled eggs

Wash, trim, and steam the beans. Leave to cool

Scrub and cook the potatoes. Leave to cool.

Wash and coarsely chop the spring onions.

Wash, dry, and chop the tarragon.

Stir the saffron into the mayonnaise.

Cut the beans into 2.5cm OR 1-inch lengths.

Halve or quarter the potatoes, depending on their size.

Shell and quarter the eggs lengthways.

Combine all the ingredients, and enjoy!

A vegetarian treat that offers plenty of aphrodisiac qualities

Vegetable timbale

I first ate these delicious and very professional-looking towers of vegetables in a tiny café overlooking Lake Zurich, the German-speaking part of Switzerland which is a wonderful place to eat healthy salads and vegetables.

Surprisingly, this nutritious vegetarian treat is also excellent sex food. It contains masses of betacarotene, lots of vitamin E, plenty of good, energy-giving calories, and the traditional stimulus of pepper – all of which add to its aphrodisiac qualities.

2 large carrots

Half a celeriac

2 medium beetroot

400g OR 14oz cooked basmati rice

2 tablespoons finely chopped fresh flat-leaved parsley

1 tablespoon finely snipped fresh chives

Freshly ground black pepper

2 tablespoons extra-virgin olive oil

A few whole fresh chives

Wash, trim, peel, and grate the vegetables.

Thoroughly mix the grated vegetables with the cooked rice.

Add all the chopped herbs, pepper, and olive oil, and mix again.

Firmly press the mixture into four timbale pots. Refrigerate for at least an hour before serving.

Turn out onto a plate and garnish with the whole chives, or more parsley if preferred.

Packed with zinc and fatty acids for ultimate performance

Casanova's salad

Casanova was reputed to eat seventy oysters a day – usually while sharing a bath with his latest paramour. If you had to open seventy oysters, you'd have no need of any aphrodisiacs as, unless you're one of those amazing men behind the shellfish counters of Paris, you'd have no time for anything else.

All shellfish are aphrodisiacs because they're rich in zinc, which is essential for male sexual performance, and essential fatty acids, which are good for both sexes. *Vongole* are wonderful baby clams, widely used in the Mediterranean. Nothing could be simpler, healthier, or more delicious than this salad, dedicated to the greatest lover of all time.

1 kg OR 2lb 4oz fresh vongole (baby clams)

500g OR 1lb 2oz new potatoes

2 knobs of unsalted butter

1 small onion, peeled and finely chopped

1 glass of dry white wine

1 bunch of fresh flat-leaved parsley, washed and chopped

Freshly ground black pepper

Wash the vongole, discarding any open ones.

Scrub, but don't peel, the potatoes and put them on to cook.

Put the vongole into a saucepan with 1cm OR half-inch of water in the bottom.

Cover tightly and boil briskly for five minutes.

Line a sieve with a double layer of kitchen muslin. Strain the vongole, returning the liquid to the saucepan.

Add a knob of butter to the pan, along with the onion.

Bring to the boil, add the white wine, and boil until reduced by half.

When the potatoes are cooked, strain and toss in the remaining butter as well as the chopped parsley.

Add the vongole to the potatoes, season with pepper, and pour the wine sauce over the top. Serve warm.

A naturally stimulating feast for all the senses

Ultimate aphrodisia

No other vegetable is imbued with such a tradition of aphrodisiac qualities as asparagus. This is one old wives' tale that works, and it isn't just because of the imagery or the sense of extravagant indulgence, since asparagus contains natural stimulating chemicals. Add the vitamin E from the olive oil, together with iron and protein from the egg, and you have a salad that's a feast for the eyes, succour to the soul…and I'll leave the rest to your imagination.

24 spears of fresh asparagus

4 hard-boiled eggs

4 tablespoons extra-virgin olive oil

1 tablespoon balsamic vinegar

A generous mound of very thin Parmesan shavings

Wash and cook the asparagus. Drain and leave to cool.

Shell and chop the eggs.

Whisk together the olive oil and balsamic vinegar.

Put six asparagus spears on each plate. Sprinkle the tips with the hard-boiled eggs and shavings of Parmesan.

Drizzle with the dressing – and let nature take its course.

A sensual salad with a symbolic twist

Quail's nest

I'd never eaten quail's eggs until 1969, when I spent Easter weekend in a beautiful hotel near Hilversum, in Holland. It had been a royal palace and was set in stunning grounds. As I sat in the elegant dining room for breakfast on Easter morning, they served this traditional Dutch Easter breakfast. I think it was meant more as a religious symbol than an aphrodisiac, but it serves both purposes.

As mentioned previously, eggs are the ultimate symbol of fertility, and when put together with the sexually stimulating mustard oils in the cress, this is not a dish I'd recommend for breakfast – unless you have the morning off!

1 dozen quail's eggs

3 packs of growing cress

2 sticks of celery, preferably with leaves

10 radishes

2 tablespoons standard salad dressing (*see* page 7)

Celery salt

Hard-boil the quail's eggs (not more than five minutes.)

Shell the eggs.

Snip the cress from the packs.

Wash the celery, cut into 2.5cm OR 1-inch chunks, and slice into batons. Chop any leaves.

Wash and thinly slice the radishes.

Make a nest of cress on each plate. Surround it with the celery and radishes.

Put three eggs in the centre of each nest and drizzle a little dressing over the salad.

Put a pile of celery salt on the edge of each plate – it's the traditional accompaniment to quail's eggs.

Sprinkle with the chopped celery leaves.

Salad

Hea

The idea of using food as medicine goes back to man's earliest days. The Chinese wrote about it 5,000 years ago, while the ancient Persian Ebers papyrus, written in 2500 BC, contains specific instructions concerning the healing use of food. For example, as a remedy for night blindness, it recommends eating roasted and crushed ox liver.

These ancient physicians didn't know that ox liver is the richest source of vitamin A, or that a deficiency of this nutrient was the main cause of night blindness. Yet their lack of understanding of the mechanisms of the illness didn't prevent them from using this "kitchen medicine" prescription, which certainly would have helped address the problem.

Today, thankfully, we know far more about the role nutritional influences play in disease. In the following pages you will find a very simple guide to using your own kitchen as nature's pharmacy. There are no prescriptions here, no visits to the doctor, no waiting at the chemist; just a wide range of delicious foods that you can incorporate into this book's huge selection of recipes for making wonderful and beneficial salads.

All fruits, vegetables, nuts, seeds, meat, fish, and poultry contain a host of natural chemicals that add to the nutritional value of everything you eat, and these nutrients are essential for good health. In addition, however, there are phytochemicals – chemical substances found naturally in plants – which have specific therapeutic benefits. This is neither a new nor a radical concept. When you rinse your mouth with the pink liquid at the dentist, for example, it contains a strong antiseptic called thymol, a substance that occurs naturally in the herb thyme, which is where it was first discovered.

Similarly, as mentioned earlier in this book, the ancient Greeks used extracts made from wild lettuce as a sleeping potion. Whenever you cut the stalk of a lettuce, a sticky, white substance comes out; this contains morphine-like chemicals that are powerfully hypnotic. All modern lettuces are descended from the original wild variety of lettuce and contain tiny amounts of the same chemical; for this reason, a late-night lettuce sandwich or a mixed green salad is a good alternative to over-the-counter sleeping pills – and it has far fewer unwanted side effects.

Indeed, food is the most natural of medicines, able to help relieve a whole host of different ills. That is why in this section you'll find help for acne and anaemia, cholesterol and coughs, gallstones and gingivitis, heartburn and herpes, menstrual problems, and mouth ulcers, and even varicose veins. Of course, eating a salad won't cure serious health problems, so always consult your healthcare professional about any condition that causes concern. Yet as part of a general health regime, specific salads will help alleviate specific problems. Even if you're already taking prescribed medication, adding the appropriate foods to your daily diet will speed your recovery in a gentle, natural, and non-invasive way.

Salad Healing Charts

Condition	Ingredients	Effect
Acne	Dandelion	Cleansing and diuretic
	Fennel	Stimulates the liver and improves fat digestion
	Garlic	Rich in antibacterial compounds
Anaemia	Chicory, watercress, dates	All are good sources of iron
Anxiety	Basil	Contains mood-enhancing linalool
	Rosemary	A traditional brain-booster
	Buckwheat	Improves blood flow to the brain
Arthritis	Cabbage	Contains healing mucilage
	Celery, turnips	Stimulate and eliminate the excretion of uric acid
	Mussels	Contain anti-inflammatory oils
	Dandelion leaves	Are strongly diuretic and cleansing
Asthma	Garlic, onions	Are both antibacterial; garlic also reduces mucus
	Carrots	Contain lung-healing betacarotene
	Lemon juice	Provides protective vitamin C and bioflavonoids
Back pain	Thyme	Supplies muscle-relaxing volatile oils
	Radishes	Contain pain-relieving mustard oils
	Walnuts	Are rich in anti-inflammatory oils
Bronchitis	Onions, chives	Sources of antibacterial sulphur compounds
	Coriander	Contains coriandrol, a natural decongestant
	Asparagus	A gentle diuretic that relieves congestion
Catarrh	Garlic	Provides antibacterial sulphur compounds
	Leeks	An effective decongestant
	Parsley	Is strongly diuretic

Condition	Ingredients	Effect
Chilblains	Basil, chives, coriander, chilli	All contain vitamins and phytochemicals which help stimulate circulation
Cholesterol	Garlic	Supplies the phytochemical allicin, which eliminates cholesterol
	Chives	Lower cholesterol, like all members of the onion family
	Olive oil	Supplies monounsaturated fats that reduce cholesterol
	Beans	Supply soluble fibre that lowers cholesterol
Chronic fatigue	Basil	Contains mood-enhancing volatile oils
	Almonds	Are a rich source of energy, protein, B vitamins, and zinc
	Beetroot, chicory	Both are blood-builders, cleansers, and tonic detoxifiers
Circulation problems	Chives, coriander	Both stimulate the circulation
	Cabbage	A rich source of mustard oils which help speed blood flow
	Buckwheat	Contains rutin, which strengthens blood vessels
	Mackerel	Provides essential fatty acids, essential for healthy circulation
Colds	Garlic	A rich source of antibacterial and antiviral sulphur compounds
	Thyme	Contains thymol, a powerful antiseptic
	Blueberries	A powerful protective package of antioxidants
	Oranges, kiwi fruit	For vitamin C; kiwi fruit also supplies vitamin E and betacarotene
Constipation	Dandelion leaves	Supply phytochemicals that stimulate the colon
	Celeriac, pulses, raisins	Are all rich in fibre to promote regularity
	Live yoghurt	Contains beneficial bacteria for good digestion
Cough	Garlic, turnips	Are antibacterial
	Thyme	An antibacterial and expectorant
	Watercress	Contains benzyl oils, which are antibacterial, and other phytochemicals that protect lung tissue
Cystitis	Parsley	A gentle diuretic, which maintains a good flow of urine
	Pumpkin seeds	A rich source of zinc – important for the urinary system
	Sage	Contains volatile oils which are a urinary antiseptic
	Asparagus	Provides the kidney stimulant asparagine; use the cooking water in soups and sauces

Condition	Ingredients	Effect
Depression	Basil	Helps the anxiety that often accompanies depression
	Buckwheat	Contains rutin, which helps lift depression and promote energy
	Apples	Are rich in nutrients with physical and mental tonic effects
	Leeks	Rich in potassium and powerfully cleansing for mind and body
Diarrhoea	Mint	An effective antacid, which helps settle the stomach
	Garlic	For diarrhoea caused by food poisoning
	Apples	Contain malic acid, which soothes the stomach lining
	Rice	A traditional eastern treatment for diarrhoea
Diverticulitis	Sage	Astringent and cleansing to the gut
	Mint	An effective antacid that helps settle the stomach
	Live yoghurt	Provides beneficial bacteria for better digestion
	Lentils	For essential bulk and soluble fibre
Flatulence	Fennel	Contains fenchone, which relieves wind (and colic in children)
	Mint	A traditional digestive aid that relieves flatulence
	Caraway seeds	Added to cabbage and beans – phytochemicals stop flatulence
Fluid retention	Parsley, dandelion, leaves, celery	All are effective natural diuretics
Gallstones	Radishes	Contain natural chemicals that stimulate the gall bladder
	Tarragon	Contains volatile oils that improve liver function
	Pineapple	Provides bromelain to counteract inflammation
Gingivitis	Lemon	Super-rich in vitamin C for healthy gums
	Sage	Cleansing and strongly antibacterial
	Thyme	Provides the antiseptic chemical thymol
	Apples	Massage the gums and promote healing
Gout	Dandelion tea	A diuretic that helps remove uric acid
	Olive oil	A rich source of monounsaturated fats which ease joint pain
	Strawberries	Reduce uric acid levels and relieve pain
	Sauerkraut	Anti-arthritic, with natural bacteria that boost immunity
Hair problems	Prawns	Very rich in zinc, which is essential for healthy hair
	Pumpkin seeds	One of the best plant sources of zinc

Condition	Ingredients	Effect
	Avocado	An excellent source of vitamin E
	Horseradish	Helps improve circulation to the scalp
Halitosis	Anise, dill, fennel, seeds, parsley	All freshen the breath
	Celery	Contains fibrous tissue to massage the gums and protect against gingivitis, a common cause of breath problems
Headache	Tofu	Contains plant hormones which help regulate the menstrual cycle and relieve headaches associated with PMS
	Dandelion leaves	A diuretic for headaches caused by fluid retention
	Radishes	A liver cleanser for headaches caused by over-indulgence
Heart disease	Garlic	Lowers blood pressure and cholesterol as well as reducing the stickiness of the blood. Eat at least one whole clove daily in food
	Dandelion leaves	A diuretic that protects against high blood pressure
	Blueberries	A heart-protective antioxidant, so use regularly
	Apples	Two a day will lower cholesterol levels
	Beans	Provide soluble fibre, which lowers cholesterol
	Oatmeal	Contains soluble fibre and vitamin E for a healthy heart
	Whitebait	Like all oily fish, they contain heart-protective fatty acids, but no damaging saturated fats
Heartburn	Mint	The most effective remedy of all; a glass of mint tea sweetened with a little honey after each meal and at bedtime will help relieve heartburn almost instantly
Hepatitis	Globe artichoke	Stimulates the function of the gall bladder and improves liver function
	Chicory	Contains bitter natural substances that stimulate liver and digestion functions
	Tarragon	Exerts beneficial effects on the liver and gall bladder and should be added to food
Herpes	Lemon balm	Is specifically antiviral; add it to any of the salads
	Garlic	Strongly antiviral; eat at least one whole clove a day

Condition	Ingredients	Effect
Hypertension	Garlic	Lowers blood pressure and cholesterol as well as reducing the stickiness of the blood. Eat at least one whole clove daily
	Parsley	A good diuretic that lowers blood pressure
	Tomatoes	Rich in lycopene, an antioxidant which protects the heart and blood vessels
	Lentils	Contain a special type of fibre that helps control blood pressure
	Tofu	Rich in plant hormones that help lower blood pressure
Indigestion	Mint	The most effective remedy of all. Add to salads, but a glass of mint tea sweetened with a little honey after each meal and at bedtime helps relieve indigestion almost instantly
	Fennel	An excellent remedy for indigestion
	Apples	Rich in malic acid, an effective antacid
Influenza	Blueberries	Rich in vitamin C and antioxidants
	Watercress	Rich in antiviral mustard oils and lung-protective phytochemicals
	Carrots	Contain huge amounts of immune-boosting betacarotene
	Yoghurt	Provides beneficial bacteria that stimulate immunity
Insomnia	Lettuce	Contains tiny amounts of morphine-like chemicals
	Chickpeas	Contain calcium and tryptophan, both sleep-inducers
	Basil	Supplies volatile oils which are calming and relaxing
	Pasta	A good source of sleep-inducing tryptophan
Laryngitis	Sage	Contains the antibacterial volatile oil thujone
	Pineapple	A rich source of bromelain, effective in the relief of sore throats
	Leeks	Contain many natural antibacterial chemicals
Menstrual problems	Tofu	Rich in natural isoflavones, which help regulate hormone levels
	Dates	Provide iron to combat anaemia
	Olive oil	Rich in vitamin E, which helps reduce menstrual discomfort
	Pumpkin seeds	Supply zinc and vitamin E which help menstrual problems
	Wholemeal bread	For B vitamins, all important for normal menstruation
Mouth ulcers	Garlic	Is strongly antibacterial and antiviral
	Thyme	Supplies the natural healing antiseptic oil thymol

Condition	Ingredients	Effect
Obesity	Parsley, dandelion leaves	Are both effective natural diuretics
	Pasta, rice, potatoes	All excellent as part of a weight-loss regime; they're filling, nourishing, sustaining, and fat-free
	Fish	Rich in minerals and protein; the oily varieties contain essential fatty acids; no saturated fat but lots of healthy nutrients
Raynaud's disease	Basil, chives, coriander	All contain vitamins and phytochemicals which help stimulate circulation; add to as many salads as possible
	Horseradish, chillies	Provide powerful circulatory stimulants
	Ginger	Contains the essential oil gingerol, which also stimulates blood flow to the tiniest blood vessels in the hands and feet
Restless legs	Chicken livers	Rich in iron to prevent anaemia, a common cause of restless legs
	Tomatoes	Provide potassium to prevent cramp
	Herrings	Rich in essential fatty acids, which improve circulation
	Onions	Help reduce cholesterol and improve blood flow
Seasonal Affective Disorder (SAD)	Basil	Helps the anxiety that often accompanies seasonal affective disorder; add to salads and sandwiches
	Bread, potatoes, rice, oats, pasta	All good sources of complex carbohydrates, which help maintain even blood-sugar levels and reduce the ups and downs of SAD
	Vongole (baby clams)	A rich source of zinc, essential to fight the chronic fatigue that goes with SAD
Sinusitis	Horseradish, chillies	Contain volatile oils that simulate and clear the sinuses
	Papayas	Contain healing enzymes that benefit all mucous membranes
	Cabbage	Rich in antibacterial sulphur compounds which fight infection
	Kiwi fruit	A rich source of immune-boosting vitamin C
Varicose veins	Basil, chives, coriander	All contain vitamins and phytochemicals, which help stimulate circulation; use generously in salads
	Chillies	Rich in capsaicin, which stimulates and improves circulation
	Nuts and seeds	Contain vitamin E, important for the health of blood vessels

Index